The Search, Source, and Signs of *Satisfaction*

DEEPER

still

AUSTIN MCNEIL

LUCIDBOOKS

Deeper Still
The Search, Source, and Signs of Satisfaction

Published by Lucid Books in Houston, TX
www.lucidbookspublishing.com

eISBN: 978-1-63296-787-9
ISBN: 978-1-63296-785-5 (Paperback)
ISBN: 978-1-63296-786-2 (Hardback)

Special Sales: Most Lucid Books titles are available in special quantity discounts. Custom imprinting or excerpting can also be done to fit special needs. For standard bulk orders, go to www.lucidbooksbulk.com. For specialty press or large orders, contact Lucid Books at books@lucidbookspublishing.com.

To Rowan and Lochlan;
May you ever drink from the Well that never runs dry.

Oh, that men would give thanks to the
Lord for His goodness,
And for His wonderful works to the children of men!
For He satisfies the longing soul,
And fills the hungry soul with goodness.

—Ps. 107:8–9

TABLE OF CONTENTS

INTRODUCTION

*The whole life of man until he is converted to Christ
is a ruinous labyrinth of wanderings.*
                                              —John Calvin

There is no heartache like that of disappointment. There are certainly deeper hurts and darker trials, but the pangs of a dissatisfied life are thorough and numbing. I know that from personal experience. There have been seasons of my life when I have felt empty—moments when every-thing I trusted to supply me with fulfillment and satisfaction proved to be incapable of ever holding such a treasure. Whether it was from premature overcommitment in relationships or misguided attempts to create identity, I know too well of disappointment's sting and consequential sense of lostness. Thankfully, the grace of God intervened and used those moments to usher me toward Jesus. I've since discovered the fullness of the life He offers.

However, even after dealing with my own disappointments, I vividly recall the secondhand hurt I experienced throughout young adulthood as I watched my friends walk through cycles of their own dissatisfaction. Time and time again, I witnessed them wander into what theologian John Calvin called the "ruinous labyrinth"—that maze of a quest for satisfaction. Some of my friends poured their lives into education, hoping that a degree would offer fulfillment and satisfaction. Others aimed for the get-rich-quick lifestyle, thinking that if they just had money, life would be everything they dreamed. For others, it was relationships, sex, or substance. Some were literally living just for the weekend. It seemed that everyone was searching in different places, but no one knew where to find the life they all wanted.

Young adulthood has become the quintessential trial phase. It's said to be the time when we should experiment, cut loose, try new things, and simply figure out who we are. A few mistakes along the way are normal and harmless, or so we hope. You only live once, so make it count, right? This aspiration for freedom seemingly promises satisfaction. The only problem is that this philosophy is proving unquestionably false.

Recent Harvard-led surveys reveal that Millennials and Gen Zers are scoring the lowest of any adult generation in the categories of happiness, life satisfaction, and meaningfulness. In fact, Gen Zers scored the lowest in every category of well-being with Millennials not far behind. According to research, young adults ages 18 to 25 are currently the least-satisfied generation on earth. What is so striking is that this same survey conducted 22 years ago revealed that middle-aged adults were the least satisfied in life while young adults were scoring relatively much higher, even among the highest.

Clearly something is off. We are the most technologically advanced, globally connected generation the world has ever seen. Our most prominent philosophers tell us that our purpose in life is whatever we make it out to be. Meanwhile, our most influential celebrities tell us that life is found in having a good time. It doesn't sound complicated—do what makes you happy, and that's where you will find true life. But if that were true, why are we so dissatisfied?

To put it bluntly, it's because they're wrong. While these notions may make for catchy lyrics or entertaining TV, they also make for worlds of heartbreak and lifetimes of scars. And they never leave us truly satisfied. But what if young adulthood didn't have to be an elaborate trial? What if we didn't have to spend those years searching? What if—regardless of who we marry, what we study, or where we work—we could live with a sense of satisfaction and fulfillment right now?

It's my aim that by the end of this book, you'll not only realize that satisfaction exists but will know where to look for it and what it looks like in your life. So whether you're still searching, mostly skeptical, or spiritually stuck, this is for you.

part one

THE SEARCH FOR SATISFACTION

The woman said to him, "Sir, give me this water, so that I will not be thirsty or have to come here to draw water."

—John 4:15 (NET)

~ *chapter one* ~

FROM FOUNTAIN TO FAKES

I was on my way to work one beautiful fall morning (in Texas that means "Summer: The Reunion Tour") when the strangest event took place. As I was driving through the parking lot of my apartment complex, a middle-aged woman came running out, yelling and waving at a car that had just pulled out onto the street. It was one of those situations where your eyes get big but your head goes down. You want to see what's happening, but you're not necessarily volunteering to get involved. Hoping it was just a mom's dramatic attempt to give her kid their forgotten lunchbox, I slowly but surely tried to continue driving.

As I got closer to her, she immediately turned from the car she was chasing and started looking for the next closest person. Well, the next closest person just happened to be me and my 2001 Ford F-150. Sure enough, she started waving me down.

At that point, I'd like to say that an extraordinary sense of Christlike compassion compelled me to stop, but what choice did I have when a woman was standing in the parking lot right in front of my truck?

As I stopped, she approached my truck from the passenger side. Remember, I'm driving a 2001 Ford pickup. This thing doesn't have power windows but rather a world-class, cutting-edge technology called a manual window crank. It's that thing that makes you feel like you're churning butter every time you go through a drive-through. To this day, the world hasn't discovered a better forearm workout. Unfortunately, these window cranks make it impossible to conveniently roll down your passenger-side window from the driver's seat. Knowing that I love pizza rolls a little too much to possess the military-grade stamina required to lean all the way over and roll down the window for this woman, I made the mistake of opening the passenger door entirely. Before I knew it, she was halfway in my truck, saying, "That was my Uber. We've got to catch it."

Look, I'm well aware of stranger danger. I've watched way too many *Criminal Minds* episodes to be handing out free rides to anyone who jumps in my truck. But here is the problem: When she said, "That was my Uber. We've got to catch it," all I could hear was "car chase." So before my adult self could say "I don't know about this," my inner child had already said, "Let's go."

Next thing I know, she's in the passenger seat, and we are racing off to catch her Uber. Feeling like I had just been cast for *Fast and Furious 57* (#longestfranchiseever), I'm weaving in and out of lanes and gaining speed. If it sounds cool, don't be fooled. I'm a notoriously safe driver. All my friends make fun of me for actually driving the speed limit, which is an oddity in the state of Texas.

We can see the Uber in the distance, and we're gaining ground. In the meantime, she starts explaining the situation to me. Her car was in the shop, and she desperately needed this Uber to get to work on time. Moving beyond the excitement of the chase, I begin to understand how important catching this car is to her and her livelihood. With a renewed zeal, I push forward. A few moments pass, and we catch up to the car at a nearby stop sign. This is the moment I had been waiting for. With my head held high in a sense of accomplishment and adrenaline flowing, I pull up by the car. That's when the woman in my passenger seat utters only one, all-too-revealing word: "*Oh.*"

It wasn't the "Oh, I'm so relieved, thanks for being my hero" kind of "oh." It was very clearly an "oh" of disappointment. After she had convinced me to channel my inner Dale Earnhardt Jr., she now realized it wasn't her Uber. We had been chasing the wrong car.

So there I was—late for work and chauffeuring a random stranger who just recruited me for the world's most anti-climactic car chase. As uncomfortable as I was, I knew this woman's embarrassment and disappointment were greater. She's the one who had just flagged down a random stranger in a parking lot. And in our attempt to catch her renegade pseudo-Uber, she had missed her actual pickup time back at the apartment complex.

When I discovered that she worked nearby, I agreed to take her all the way there. We had already been through so much together, I figured I might as well see it through. I dropped her off at her job and invited her to come to my church sometime.

And that was the end of it. I've never seen her again. To this day, I have no explanation for what actually happened that morning. But the whole experience did remind me of an important truth. *Regardless of how much fun the chase can be, when you're chasing the wrong thing, you will only catch disappointment.* As exciting as the car chase felt in the moment, it ultimately proved futile and empty. The object we were chasing couldn't provide what this woman was actually seeking.

That matters, and here is why. As human beings, we are all involved in a dramatic, life-altering chase for something. In fact, most of us are chasing a lot of "somethings" in life. But there is one thing that stands above the rest and seems to encapsulate all our other desires. That is our desire for satisfaction.

When I speak of satisfaction, I don't mean materialistic wealth, life-long comfort, or social prominence. I mean something much more important. True satisfaction is contentment *in* life born from a fullness *of* life. It's knowing that you are fulfilling the purpose for which you exist.

None of us want to come to the end of our lives feeling empty and wasted. We don't want our days to be characterized by routine obligations and an unfulfilled search for joy. So what do we do? We scour every possible source for satisfaction—money, popularity, careers, degrees, friendships, spouses, sex, substance, acceptance, power, authority, comfort, and more. We run toward those things with all our energy in hopes that they will fill us with satisfaction and fulfillment.

While there isn't anything inherently wrong with most of those things, they all possess this fatal flaw: None of them can offer the satisfaction we seek. Sure, they may entertain us for a season, but whatever pleasure they offer is second-rate and fleeting. It feels a lot like chasing the wrong Uber—exciting in the moment but disappointing in the end. Despite their promising façades, all these things will ultimately leave us empty and still searching. As a result, most people spend their entire lives bouncing around from empty well to empty well in a constant search for something to fill their empty hearts.

Tale as Old as Time

This misguided search is nothing new. From the Garden of Eden to Madison Square Garden, history tells of humankind's incessant longings but consistent misdirection. Empty wells plague our fallen existence, and the people of God have proven to be no exception.

One of the clearest examples of this is found in the Old Testament book of Jeremiah. In chapter two, Jeremiah finds himself speaking on behalf of God to the people of Israel. Essentially, God is revealing to His people the grievousness of their sin. We catch a glimpse of just how grievous it is in verse 12. God is instructing all creation to be astonished, appalled, and desolate at the sight of Israel's sin. It's a very clear tone-setter. Whatever God's people have done, it's deserving the lament of all creation. So what is it they have done?

According to verse 13, their sin is twofold. First, they have forsaken God, the "fountain of living waters." I've always thought this is an interesting metaphor for God to use of Himself. While it appears simple, it's very significant. As we all know, water is absolutely necessary for life. You and I need it to survive. As much as we may try to be sustained on cold brew and Red Bull, we won't make it long without water. So when God speaks of Himself as water, it's a subtle reminder of our need of Him for survival.

And water doesn't just sustain—it satisfies. You know what it's like to jump in a pool on a hot summer day or finally drink some water after running a few laps. It's extremely refreshing and satisfying. When God refers to Himself as a fountain of living water, He is claiming to be necessary for both survival and flourishing—for sustaining our life and supplying our satisfaction. Incredibly, in the face of our foundational need for spiritual water, He offers Himself as a fountain.

Part of Israel's problem is that they have forsaken God, the fountain, but that's not all. The verse also says they have created for themselves broken cisterns that can't actually hold any water. A cistern during that time was likely either a hole in a rock that was used to catch rainwater for drinking or a pottery vessel such as a vase used to store clean water. According to the Lord, His people had abandoned Him—the fountain of living water—and were turning to broken pots that couldn't hold anything. Despite their acknowledged need for what He offered, they refused Him and attempted to satisfy their needs by their own means.

The tragedy of this passage is hard to exaggerate. Yet the resemblance of this passage to many of our lives is far more tragic. The reality is that most of our world is still looking for water in broken cisterns. We've abandoned the true source of our desires and attempted to create satisfaction in things that can never come close to comparing. As long as we do this, we will never find what we are looking for, regardless of the thrill we may find in the chase. This is how many people spend their lives—running from the fountain only to be let down by the fakes. They find themselves stuck in what feels like a never-ending search for satisfaction.

Better Places

Many of you are facing this search in monumental ways. While all ages deal with it, young adulthood proves to be a particularly difficult time in the search for satisfaction. Maybe you've just graduated from high school and are trying to determine what to do with your life. Maybe you're in the middle of your degree and facing serious doubts about whether you've made the right decision. Maybe you've been in the work force for years and yet still have no sense of direction. We're all asking the same question: *What should I be doing with my life that will give it satisfaction, fulfillment, and meaning?* While I can't offer you specific details about jobs or romances, I do pray that you will be able to form a foundation through this study on which you can build a satisfying life.

Remember this: Your desire for satisfaction in life is both justifiable and achievable. Some of you may have already given up on the search. You've been hurt too many times or been left feeling empty too often. Some of you may even feel shame for admitting that you're still searching. But know that you are not wrong or immoral to have such desires, and neither is your search pointless or futile.

You have been created with both the desire for satisfaction and the capacity to be satisfied. It is part of the design that was instilled in you by your Creator. As we will see more clearly, these deep longings serve not only as intrinsic evidences of a

Creator but also as intended motivations for you to pursue Him. God has instilled this longing within us that it might lead us to what truly satisfies—God (see Psalm 107:9 and 145:16 for starters).

The issue is not that our desire for satisfaction exists; it's that we, with our desire, chase after and settle for the wrong things. The famed 20th century theologian C. S. Lewis put it this way:

> It would seem that our Lord finds our desires not too strong, but too weak. We are half-hearted creatures, fooling about with drink and sex and ambition when infinite joy is offered us, like an ignorant child who wants to go on making mud pies in a slum because he cannot imagine what is meant by the offer of a holiday at the sea. We are far too easily pleased.

Mud pies in the slum versus a vacation on the beach? I think I know which one I'd choose. Yet time and time again, we settle for the mud. Lewis' last phrase hauntingly summarizes our world—*"We are far too easily pleased."* Our problem isn't that we long for satisfaction; it's that we are too easily pleased with things that can never actually satisfy.

The invitation of this study is simple. Don't settle for passing pleasures when complete satisfaction is available. Stop playing with mud and venture into the wonder of the beach. Ditch the cisterns and head back to the Fountain. Don't stop looking for satisfaction; just start looking in better places.

~ *chapter two* ~

NEVER THIRST AGAIN

Christianity is no stranger to human longing. The pages of Scripture are filled with real stories of people just like you and me who know what it's like to endure deep seasons of longing for satisfaction. From David's emotional outpourings in the Psalms to the Apostle Paul's dramatic deferment to the eternal in his epistles, the Bible oozes of those yearning for more. But when it comes to empty attempts at fulfillment and their consequential distress, no one understands better than the woman spoken of in John 4. She is famously nicknamed "the Woman at the well" and is one of Jesus's most memorable interactions.

....

At this point, it would be really helpful to put this book down and read the account in John 4:3–43. Seriously, do it!

....

It all starts as Jesus is making His way from Judea, the southern portion of Israel, to Galilee, the northern region where He spent His childhood. Sandwiched between these two regions was Samaria, a place of much contention and the home of the despised Samaritans. Jesus, choosing to journey through Samaria, stops to rest at a local water well. It certainly isn't the beaver-branded paradise of Buc-ee's, but it would have been a welcomed reprieve from the Middle Eastern sun. While Jesus is at this well, His disciples head into town to grab some food, leaving Jesus the perfect opportunity to initiate a conversation with a local woman who had come to draw water. It quickly becomes clear that this is no chance interaction. It isn't the product of timely coincidence. Jesus planned on being there at that moment, in that spot, with that woman. Why? Because Jesus knew she was harboring a lifetime of failures and unfulfilled longings. He knew she was searching.

The Searching Woman

The most notable detail about this woman at the well is her romantic history. If we dare to venture beyond that, we find that she has a whole ensemble of sad stories and social hangups. Her story is more than failed lovers and bad breakups. It appears from the context and her comments that at this point in her life, nothing is going her way. Take note of a few of her primary characteristics.

She is Socially Disdained. The conversation begins by Jesus asking the woman for a drink of water. That's not a big deal, right? Well, apparently it is. She simply looks at Jesus and says, "Why are you talking to me?" While this response is certainly defensive, it doesn't quite qualify her for the cast of *Mean Girls*. The truth is, Jesus is breaking multiple cultural boundaries just by speaking with her, and she is shocked.

First off, their being opposite genders creates a problem. In first-century Palestine, public conversations between males and females were considered largely inappropriate. Secondly, she is a Samaritan, and Jesus is a Jew. These two people groups treated each other with the utmost contempt due to a long history of differences. To Samaritans, Jews were the better-than-everyone-else religious snobs of the day. To Jews, the Samaritans were considered half-breeds who had compromised their faith and culture through mixed marriages with foreign people and had built an illegitimate temple (see John 4:20). It's no surprise that this woman can't withhold her shock when Jesus initiates a conversation. They are at opposite ends of deep cultural rifts.

More than the mere customs and taboos of the day, the woman demonstrates an additional degree of cultural segregation by showing up at the well at 12:00 noon, the hottest part of the day. The hot, Middle Eastern sun is at its peak and nearly unbearable. That's why most women traveled together in groups to draw water early in the morning before it was too hot. So why would this woman be drawing water in the middle of the day? It's simple. She wants to avoid people. It is highly likely that she has been outcast by the other women of her community due to her sexual promiscuity. Her colored romantic past had won her a scarlet letter for adultery, a label that also rendered her religiously unclean.

Clearly, this woman is used to avoiding conversation and people all together. Her first response to Jesus's inquiry is one of surprise and confusion. Why? Because she isn't used to people acknowledging her, at least not in meaningful ways. She is accustomed to exclusion from the religious, contempt from the Jews, and disdain from the Samaritans. So - what could this wandering Jewish rabbi possibly want with her?

She is Superficially Disguised. Jesus, having a limited amount of time and a very clear objective, completely disregards her cultural hangups and conversational shock. In fact, He doesn't even answer her question about why He is talking to her. He simply tells her that if she only knew who He was and the gift God is extending, she'd be asking Him for water. Talk about a dramatic and confusing escalation in the conversation! Jesus sounds like He needs some shade and a Gatorade. This woman may have been suspecting heatstroke. Which is why the woman calls into question both the logical viability of Jesus's offer and the self-assumed greatness of Jesus's statement.

Seeing through these conversational distractions, Jesus presses further into the mess. He tells her that He can offer her living water. And for the first time in the conversation, the woman doesn't respond defensively. She doesn't ask questions or offer diversions. Though not yet understanding the spiritual significance, she finally offers a glimpse of her true longing by saying, "Sir, give me this water, so that I will not be thirsty or have to come here to draw water" (John 4:15). She's thinking this could entirely eliminate her midday walk of shame to the water well.

Perfect, right? Isn't this exactly the place Jesus is trying to get her to? She has acknowledged that, at least to some degree, and she wants what He is offering. Any good salesperson knows that this would be the time to seal the deal. Luckily for us, Jesus isn't a salesman. His concern is the transformation of our lives, not the gaining of our business. That's why Jesus does the least salesman-like thing by bringing up her romantic life. He asks her to go and get her husband.

This is a really complicated request for the woman, though she attempts to play it off as if it weren't. In a seemingly straightforward answer, the woman declares that she has no husband. Which, though factually correct, doesn't tell the whole story. As Jesus supernaturally points out, the woman had already been married five times to five different men. Apparently, the marriages had all failed because she was now living with her most recent boyfriend, which qualified as adultery.

So did she technically have a husband? Well, no, not at that moment. But she'd had five of them throughout her life. And now it seems she's abandoned all hope in the institution of marriage and is trying that "friends with benefits" kind of life. While her answer may have qualified as the truth for an online relationship status, it clearly lacked fullness of honesty. In fact, in many ways, it was a disguise.

Behind her husbandless confession was a world of intense hurt—a hidden history of failed love and empty wells, an all-too-familiar sting of constant disappointments. As our culture knows all too well, divorce is an ugly, painful thing. One divorce is enough to inflict a lifetime of pain. But five of them? Whatever pieces of this woman's heart that remains intact is no doubt going to be guarded and impenetrable.

That's why she tells Jesus she doesn't have a husband. It's easier to hide the baggage of hurt and appear a little less broken. She doesn't really know this guy. Full disclosure of her romantic timeline is likely to send Him running away, just as most everyone else had done. So it's easier to give Him something factually correct but a little less than the truth. The only flaw in this subtle disguise is that Jesus had already seen through it. And in what had to have been the most uncomfortable moment of this woman's life, Jesus reveals that He knows every second of her past.

Can you imagine that moment? We all have things about our past that we wouldn't share with close friends, much less a random stranger. Sins we've struggled with, failures we've experienced, disappointments we've endured—those aren't exactly our favorite conversational icebreakers with the barista at Starbucks. We keep those things tucked away inside. Should they surface, we know they will only bring us shame and embarrassment. We hide our guilt and shame behind carefully constructed images and technically true facts that are designed to satisfy the curious but guard from any authentic transparency. Just like this woman, we stick to the shallow side of our past because the truth often feels too deep to swim in. The amazing thing is that even though this woman tried to disguise her brokenness, Jesus already knew all about it. And without balk or hesitancy, Jesus still pursues her.

She is Spiritually Deferred. Immediately, the woman admits that Jesus must be a prophet. This declaration sounds like a discovery belonging more to Captain Obvious than to Sherlock Holmes. It probably wasn't too hard to deduce after the awkward "I-know-about-your-exes" monologue. If Jesus isn't a representative of God, she should probably be considering a restraining order at this point because He clearly knows way more than any normal person should.

Having recognized that Jesus was clearly involved with the divine, the woman attempts to divert the conversation from her now-blurted-out past. She poses a theological question that is sure to spark debate and remove her dating life from center stage. She asks Jesus about the proper place to worship—again, a source of major contention between the Jews and the Samaritans. Unlike her other diversions, Jesus goes along with this one. He offers her some transformational insight into the nature of true worship and what is pleasing to God. But pay attention to what she says next.

Likely caught off guard by Jesus's non-run-of-the-mill answer, the woman chooses to defer on the topic rather than continue. She says, "I know the Messiah is coming. . . . When He comes, He will tell us all things" (John 4:25). Translation: "I don't know about all that; I guess we'll just have to wait for the Messiah." Rather than offer a defense, she defers to the future. She looks ahead to a time when, because of the Messiah, all will be made clear, and all will be made whole.

Like the rest of Israel, she is desperately waiting for this Promised One of God. His arrival will secure clarity of truth, finality of righteousness, and restoration of brokenness. Her deferment is not without its virtue. However, this deferment reveals a painful irony. She is so used to deferring her hope to the future that she doesn't recognize the fulfillment of her hope that is standing right before her.

Have you ever been there? Within you is a hope that things won't always be the way they are. But time goes by, and what you've hoped for seems no closer than it was a year ago. Every passing day wearies your heart and strains your hope. The truth is that the longer you wait for something to arrive, the more disappointed you grow in its absence. As Solomon said in Proverbs 13:12, "Hope deferred makes the heart sick." Historically, much of Israel has felt this deferred sickness. For centuries they have waited for this Messiah, yet they have been seemingly left in their hope. Imagine how this woman must have felt after years of broken hearts and empty wells.

Gratefully, Scripture leaves no room for imagination. We know how she is feeling. Based on what we've just discovered, she is feeling outcast, empty, disdained, and deferred. If satisfaction in life exists, she has never tasted it. That's why the offer of Jesus seems to resonate. When she hears Jesus mention a living water that springs up to eternal life, her immediate demand is to give her this water. She's tired of being thirsty and coming to this well. She longs for something more, something that will override her current embarrassment and satisfy her still unmet need for fulfillment. Even if she hasn't connected all the dots quite yet, she is longing for living water.

The Satisfying Savior

Despite her broken past and current social distress, Jesus offers the woman at the well a chance to partake of living water. That offer admittedly sounds way too good to be true and slightly confusing. However, what I love about this interaction is that Jesus demonstrates an immense amount of shepherding just to draw her to the point of understanding.

After side-stepping her cultural hesitancy, Jesus says, "If you knew the gift of God, and who it is who says to you, 'Give Me a drink,' you would have asked Him, and He would have given you living water" (John 4:10). Despite our tendency to read it with a tone of condescension, Jesus is actually outlining His conversational points. He is essentially saying, "If you knew A (the Gift of God) and B (who I am), you'd be asking for C (living water)." He knows the woman already desires this living water. The problem is that she is not fully aware of her own desire, nor does she know that Jesus can satisfy it. So He must walk her through the process in order for her to arrive at an admission of need. To get there, she needs to understand a few prerequisites—what Jesus gives and who Jesus is.

What He gives. Jesus's first prerequisite is the need to know what the gift of God is. According to Scripture, all good things are gifts from God (James 1:17). But that isn't what Jesus is speaking about. Notice the word *the* before "gift of God" in John 4:10. That word is used as a determiner in the singular sense, which means Jesus is speaking of only one particular gift, not of good gifts in general. He is being very specific.

What is Jesus referring to? Well, His explanation is a dead giveaway. Jesus says, "The water that I will give him will become in him a spring of water welling up to eternal life" (John 4:14, ESV). The gift Jesus is referring to is eternal life. Jesus was merely using their current context (a water well) to illustrate the life that God was offering this woman—a life of grace that would conquer her failures, a life of spiritual fulfillment that would overshadow her emptiness, a life of spiritual satisfaction that would one day find its consummation in an eternal dwelling place where she would forever live in the presence of her Maker and Redeemer. It is a life that never truly ends, even if she should physically die.

This is what Jesus brings to the table for this woman. It couldn't be further from the life she's known up to this point. She doesn't yet understand what Jesus is talking about. All she knows is that she wants this water He is offering. Jesus has revealed that her deepest longings in life are actually for the eternal life God gives. Once Jesus describes it, she's in.

Who He is. When Jesus says, "If only you knew who you are talking to," it isn't an ego-motivated attempt to woo her or demand submission. He intends to spike her curiosity away from cultural rifts and toward the spiritual matter at hand. He is attempting to pique her interest in order to properly reveal His true identity.

This is exactly why He plunges into her past. He has to press into the wounds in order to reveal that He has the balm. This painful past that she is most anxious to escape just so happens to be the very place Jesus needs to reveal Himself most. And it becomes the convincing evidence that He is, in fact, the long-awaited Messiah. He displays His identity to her by demonstrating His knowledge of her. And we find that it is this exact demonstration of knowledge that convinces her that He is the Christ (John 4:26), though it isn't until He openly admits it that she fully responds (John 4:29).

It's so important that we see how these two prerequisites complement each other. It's not enough for the woman to now have specifications for her desires. This desire is pointless unless there is someone or something that can satisfy it. By revealing His divinity to her, Jesus is assuring her that he isn't selling some fountain-of-youth treasure hunt. He is who He says He is, and He can supply what she's looking for.

In her disdain, Jesus pursues her. In her disguise, Jesus sees to her. In her deferment, Jesus stands before her. When everything else has failed her, Jesus offers to fill her. To a woman who had only ever known empty wells, Jesus shows up and offers the deepest satisfaction.

Cool Story, Bro — So What?

What could a 2,000-year-old conversation around a water well possibly hold for us as we try to discern the course of our life and find fulfillment? Surprisingly, it holds a lot. While this story is a historical event rooted in a particular place in time, it holds immense spiritual implications for readers in every age.

You may have not realized it yet, but you and I are not much different than the woman at the well. Sure, we may not have quite the romantic resumé or social exclusion, but we do know what it's like to be broken. We know what it's like to lose faith in people, to hold out hope that life will get better, or to pray that we won't always feel so shattered. We know what it's like to trust that the next person, the next job, the next relationship, the next hookup, or the next paycheck will finally quench our thirst for fulfillment and satisfaction. Whether we've got the publicly visible scarlet letter or not, we know what it's like to draw from empty wells.

But the beautiful part is that Jesus's offer *still* stands. He *still* finds broken people at empty wells. He *still* offers the thirst-quenching, all-satisfying, failure-redeeming living water of eternal life. Because of who He *still* is and what He *still* gives, fullness of life is *still* available.

According to Jesus, a full, satisfied life is out there, but it's not hiding in pleasures or paychecks. Rather, *our quest for satisfaction starts and ends with Jesus.* Only Jesus can offer living water in a world of empty wells. I know this sounds like an elementary concept, especially for you seasoned churchgoers, but before you dismiss it as a cheesy bumper sticker or a clichéd slogan, understand that it truly is the foundation of the satisfied life. Its familiarity does not eliminate its truthfulness. Jesus and Jesus alone offers the life you're looking for. It may not be the life you envision, and I can guarantee it won't always be easy or trial-free, but it is the life you innately desire.

It really is this simple: true satisfaction in life begins and ends with knowing Jesus. If you have never placed your faith in who He is and what He's done for you on the cross, don't wait any longer. He's paid the debt of your sin. He's faced the wrath of God on your behalf. He's risen from the grave in power so you might have a relationship with the God for whom you were created. Apart from that, there is no lasting fulfillment in life. So put His offer to the test. Taste the living water and never thirst again.

part two

THE SOURCE OF SATISFACTION

Jesus said to her, "I who speak to you am He."
—John 4:26

~ *chapter three* ~
A TRUSTWORTHY WELL

Do you know anyone who's gullible? We've all had a momentary lapse in common sense, but I'm talking about the people who seem to live in a constant state of logical suspension. You can convince them of the most outrageous ideas just by simply stating something with confidence, making up a story to support it, and putting on a mediocre poker face. When it comes to being gullible, I've found it's a lot more fun to be in on the joke than buying into its con.

My favorite memory of my own gullibility is a direct result of my premature desire to have a beard in high school. My face falls more into the follicly-challenged category, but you'd better believe I rocked that middle school peach fuzz. As I got into high school, some of my friends grew beards full enough to convince people they held down a nine-to-five job and paid a mortgage. Yet there I was, still rocking the peach fuzz. For me, it was never about looking like a crew member of the *Black Pearl*. It was more like wanting to know I *could* grow a beard if I wanted to—a masculine principle-of-the-matter type of thing.

In my hour of desperation, I went to the best bearded man I knew—Andrew Valdez, one of my church's youth group leaders. I had known Andy for some time and had grown to respect him deeply for both his bearded abilities and his walk with Jesus. In a conversation one day, I asked him what I could do to help stimulate beard growth. I'll never forget his answer.

Andy looked at me in all his bearded glory, and with the most straight-faced seriousness he possessed, he told me I could stimulate beard growth by slicing an onion in half and rubbing the juices onto my face. Apparently, my expression showed skepticism because he quickly proceeded to explain to me why this method works. He expounded on the chemical components of onion juice and how it possessed a natural ability to open facial pores and accelerate the hair-growing process. After an embarrassingly few minutes, I believed him.

Now, before you outright put down the book and irrevocably label me an idiot, know that I did *not* actually try the onion facial. Even though I did begin to believe him, I wasn't ready to take the onion-y plunge. And in my follow-up questions, Andy had the grace to inform me that he had jokingly made up the entire thing. He didn't intend to let me actually follow through with it (at least I don't think so).

Whether you've ever rubbed onions on your face or not, you likely know what it's like to be duped into believing outrageous things. More than that, you know the fallout that can arise from placing your trust in the wrong people. That is why most of us meet big promises with even greater skepticism. The consequences of mistrust can be devastating.

Make no mistake, the entire premise of our being satisfied in Christ is built on trust. I'm not just asking you to give Him a chance for satisfaction; I'm suggesting that He is your *only* chance for it. To suggest this is to imply that you must ditch every other effort and focus on Him fully, which is both demanding and risky. If Jesus doesn't hold satisfaction, we will have wasted our lives pursuing Him when we could have been seeking other things.

This entire operation is built on trusting Him. That is why knowing Him becomes so important. Trust is born out of familiarity. The better I know someone, the more I am going to trust them. Conversely, the less I know someone, the less I will trust them. This natural law of trust impacts how we operate spiritually as well. As Jonathan Edwards once observed, "Men will trust in God no further than they know Him."

If you are going to trust Christ to provide you with satisfaction, you must know Him well enough to understand why He can provide it. We must learn to answer a foundational question: What about God earns Him the right to be trusted with our satisfaction?

The God of Our Satisfaction

Thanks to the revelation of God's Word, what was unknown through creation has become accessible through the pages of Scripture. While the universe declares His power and might, the Bible reveals His nature and heart. Among the Bible's inexhaustible descriptions of who God is, we find a recurring picture of God as the satisfier of the human heart. This manifests itself in a multitude of different ways. For the sake of our study, I'll highlight three of them.

As our Creator, offering satisfaction is one of His exclusive rights.

The Scriptures waste no time establishing where we came from and why we exist. In Genesis 1, we find the account of an eternally existing Godhead who began speaking things into existence. From the farthest corners of space to the lowest depths of the seas, every inch is the product of His willful endeavor to create a world of beauty and goodness. However, the focal point of His creative enterprise was humanity, a creation intended to bear His image and live in relationship with Him. Humanity exists as the pinnacle of His created order and the embodiment of His creative purpose.

We were made by Him. Our existence isn't a random chance or lucky coincidence. Our life is the direct result of an all-powerful God who speaks galaxies into existence and worlds into realities. We are hand-crafted and divinely animated. But more than being made *by* Him, we are also made *for* Him.

> *For by Him all things were created that are in heaven and that are on earth, visible and invisible, whether thrones or dominions or principalities or powers. All things were created through Him* and for Him. *And He is before all things, and in Him all things consist.* (emphasis added)
>
> —Col. 1:16–17

It may seem an inconsequential nuance, but it's not. To be made *by* something is to speak objectively of the created object's historical beginning. To be made *for* something is to reveal the created object's purpose and source of meaning. It's a detail that we would do well to consider.

First, to be made *for* God reveals His exclusive authority in determining the details, purposes, and bounds of our existence. Because He has made us for Himself, He is the one who decides why we exist. God owns the eternal patent on humanity. His image serves as a trademark on what is His unique, creative property. We all know what happens when a person attempts to take what someone else created and use it as their own. They get a nice, fat lawsuit typically ending with an even fatter fine. Why? Because the very act of creating something comes with a degree of ownership.

More than just establishing His exclusive authority, being made *for* God also reveals His exclusive ability to offer us the satisfaction we crave. He alone can offer what we most deeply long for because He is the One who designed us with our longings. While human sinfulness has distorted and perverted many of our desires, our innate longings for fulfillment and satisfaction are not foundationally immoral or accidental. And they aren't some elaborate tease intended to leave us on the edge with bated breath. The great English preacher Charles Spurgeon once said this:

> In spiritual things, when God has raised a desire, he always gratifies it; hence the longing is prophetic of the blessing. In no case is the desire of the living thing excited to produce distress, but in order that it may seek and find satisfaction.

God didn't create us with desires just to dangle their fulfillment out of our reach. Instead, He designed us with a desire for satisfaction and then offers Himself as its ultimate fulfillment.

Lest we confuse this point as a false attempt to make our satisfaction the primary theme of God's work, we must keep in mind that God is primarily concerned with His own glory. This was His motivation for creation. In recognizing His glory and grandeur, He sought to create a universe that would reflect His glory and praise Him for it. However, this isn't a discouraging reality that paints us as mere pawns in a game of divine self-conceitedness. God isn't arrogant for wanting the glory He is due. Rather, He chooses to make His glory known through the means of creating, sustaining, redeeming, and satisfying the human heart. You see, our satisfaction in life and His creative intents are two complementary notions that collide at His glorification. As Pastor John Piper said, "God is most glorified in us when we are most satisfied in Him." His glorification is best displayed in our satisfaction, and our satisfaction is fullest when we glorify Him.

As your Creator, God alone has the right to offer you satisfaction. He formed and shaped your innermost being, even before you ever took a breath (Ps. 139:13). There is no longing you have that He does not see. There is no desire you possess that He cannot satisfy. He alone possesses the authority and ability to offer you fullness of life.

As our Redeemer, offering satisfaction is a demonstration of His salvific might.

Jesus often described the mission of His earthly ministry. He once stated that it was to "seek and to save that which was lost" (Luke 19:10). Elsewhere He stated, "Those who are well have no need of a physician, but those who are sick. I have not come to call *the* righteous, but sinners, to repentance" (Luke 5:31–32). But of all His self-declared, ministry intentions, John 10:10 seems to resonate the deepest. In it, Jesus states that He came so "[we] might have life, and that [we] may have *it* more abundantly."

Not only do these descriptions paint an incredibly insightful picture of His ministry, but they also reveal the harsh reality of our existence without Him. He came to heal, to save, and to give life. That indicates that apart from Him, we are sick, lost, and dead. The Bible's description of the sinner's reality is comprehensibly bleak and full of dread. Sin didn't leave us wounded; it left us eternally dead. So when Jesus showed up on the scene, He wasn't offering a heavenly boost in morale. His ministry wasn't a half-time pep talk for a struggling football team. It was a daring rescue mission to redeem the enemies of God by offering His perfect life in exchange for their wretchedness. It was the most scandalous event in human history.

But notice that Jesus's aim isn't just saving us *from* something; He's also aimed at saving us *to* something. Jesus came that we may have life, not simply so we may *not* have death. He doesn't just save us *from* hell; He saves us *to* heaven. He doesn't just strip us of our sinfulness; He clothes us in His righteousness. He doesn't just absorb for us the wrath of God; He welcomes us into the family of God. He doesn't just conquer our death; He offers to us abundant life.

Generally, to have an abundance of something is to have a large, more-than-needed quantity. However, the tone of John

10:10 is meant to stress that this offered life isn't just large; it's unexpected and unanticipated. It's a life that because of our sinfulness is entirely undeserved and unattainable. So when Jesus offers life in abundance, it's nothing short of scandalous.

Contrary to most spiritualized self-help books, abundant life isn't synonymous with fame, health, and wealth. In fact, when Jesus speaks of abundant life, it isn't material or physical in nature at all. It certainly has physical implications, but those are secondary to the spiritual emphasis. Considering that the context of John 10 is that of shepherding—a concept we will develop more deeply in the next section—this reference to abundant life is most accurately expressed as an overflowing fullness of life as the result of an undeserved welcome into God's sheepfold and the unfailing provision of our Shepherd who both protects and guides His sheep. That's the life Jesus offers—an undeserved welcome that leads to an unfailing protection and provision, an eternal life overflowing with the goodness and grace of a Savior who championed our otherwise helpless cause.

We don't often think of our salvation in those terms, which is perhaps why grace so often goes underappreciated in the lives of many Christians. We fail to recognize the life that Christ has saved us to, not just the death He's saved us from. It is a life of deepest satisfaction because He is its end. A. W. Tozer effectively said it this way:

> The Church [and, by consequence, the individual Christians of whom the Church consists] will come out of her doldrums when we find out that salvation is not a lightbulb only, that it is not an

insurance policy against hell only, but that it is a gateway into God and that God is all that we would have and can desire.

Salvation is most amazing not for what it keeps us away from—namely, hell. Its greatest feat is what it invites us into—the very God in whom resides the consummation of our deepest desires.

As such, offering satisfaction and life isn't merely a right that God earned in creation; it is also a grace that He extends in salvation. It is a demonstration that He, in His goodness and might, could reach down from heaven and pull us out of the mire of our sinfulness and bring us into a life we could never have achieved on our own. Death was our rightful wage for rebellion, yet when we were most desperate and He was most justified to walk away, He chose to redeem us and offer us a new life that overflows of fullness.

As our Shepherd, offering satisfaction is the deepest of His provisional delights.

As we've already seen, one of the most prominent biblical metaphors for God's oversight of His people is shepherding. But amidst the multitude of references, none is more beloved than King David's in Psalm 23. From paraphrased references in Hollywood's biggest blockbusters to word-for-word recitations during funerals, its popularity shockingly permeates our society. Its familiarity is felt by both lifelong disciples of Jesus and those who'd never venture through the doors of a church.

Tragically, despite its familiarity in form, it mostly remains foreign in application. While many consider Psalm 23 a nice, religious sentiment, they often brush it off as mostly disconnected from their day-to-day lives. After all, when is the last time you ate grass from a pasture or were wrangled by a shepherd's staff? (If you have legitimate answers to that, I'm deeply concerned.) But while the psalm may seem out-of-touch on the surface, a closer look shows that its relevancy isn't in jeopardy. King David is actually painting a picture of the life we are all searching for—a life of satisfaction.

In fact, you'd be hard pressed to find a more comprehensive illustration of the satisfied life. David speaks of rest and restoration, of guidance and deliverance, of provision and protection, of an abundance in goodness, a faithfulness of mercy, and a lifetime of intimacy. While much study could be given to each of these nuances, you don't need a four-year degree and a full-blown exposition to uncover the Psalm's satisfactory tones. It is there from the beginning, even in the simple introduction of "The Lord is my shepherd: I shall not want" (Ps. 23:1).

The Lord's being David's Shepherd is what sets the entire tone of the passage and opens the door to the rich development of the sheep metaphor. But take note that this opening statement isn't an objective observation about God's general nature. It's a personal confession of God's unique shepherding in David's life. David said that God is *his* Shepherd in life. David isn't reciting notes from his systematic theology class; he's speaking of personal experience. It's a statement of intimacy.

David's follow-up statement of "I shall not want" is where we find our first confession of satisfaction. It should be noted that the word *want* suggests something much more than mere feelings of desire. As represented in the NET Bible, David says, that because God is his Shepherd, "[he] lacks nothing" (Ps. 23:1). The obvious implication is that as a Shepherd, God provides all that is necessary for his sheep to live and thrive. It's not a promise that the sheep get everything they want, but it does declare that they will never go without what they need. Why? Because God is a good Shepherd who delights in providing for those under His care. We see this truth multiple times throughout the Scriptures (Luke 12:32, James 1:17, Matt. 7:11).

But here is the incredible part. David's testimony of satisfaction isn't just rooted in what God tangibly provides *for* him; it's rooted in a deeper sense of understanding of who God is *to* him. David isn't just saying, "Because God is my Shepherd, I will have all I need." He is also saying, "Because God is my Shepherd, I need nothing else." There is a foundational level of satisfaction that stems not just from having what God provides but from knowing who God is. It is as if merely knowing God intimately as a personal Shepherd helped rid David of any unfulfilled longings. As a Shepherd, God doesn't just provide for our needs; He satisfies them with Himself.

What we find in these first two statements of Psalm 23 is a classic example of cause and effect. David's second confession of satisfaction is entirely dependent on the first statement of God being his Shepherd. Were you to lose intimacy with the Shepherd, you would consequently lose the satisfaction that accompanies Him. It's the personal intimacy with the Shepherd that secures the satisfaction.

The exciting truth is that God is as good a Shepherd today as He's ever been. He still delights in giving good gifts and providing fullness to His people. But it's so much deeper than grocery lists and necessities. He delights in satisfying us with Himself, as only a Shepherd could do. The question becomes not whether God has retained His ability to shepherd toward satisfaction; He has. The question is much simpler. Have you made Him your Shepherd?

God Enough and Good Enough

Here is the major takeaway from our crash course biblical survey: *God, by consequence of who He is to us and what He does for us, is entirely worthy of being trusted with our satisfaction.* I realize the stakes are high and the pressure is on. Satisfying the human heart is no simple feat. Our longings in life are deep, and no mere knockoff or counterfeit can do the trick of filling them. As Puritan theologian Thomas Brooks once said, "It is only an infinite God, and an infinite good, that can fill and satisfy the precious and immortal soul of man."

Only He who is infinitely God and infinitely good could possibly begin to satisfy. But in the face of such challenging requirements, the Scriptures present to us an exciting reality— God as glorious Creator, as gracious Redeemer, and as good Shepherd is both God enough and good enough to satisfy the human soul. All we have to do is set our eyes on and tether our hearts to His transcendent glory, His redeeming grace, and His shepherding goodness. Our longings prove deep, but He proves to be a Well deeper still. He is capable and willing. He is available and waiting. He is trustworthy of our satisfaction.

~ *chapter four* ~

THE MEANS OF DRAWING

Call it a weird flex, but one of the most subtle proofs of Western affluence is our plethora of water bottle brands. In 2023, 15.94 billion gallons of bottled water were sold in the United States. That's roughly 45 gallons per person in the country. It's no wonder that nearly every gas station has a variety of selections to choose from. They have everything from the classic off-brand cheap stuff to the bottles packaged like they were sourced on some distant planet and assembled by a team of engineers at a Tesla factory.

Unfortunately, our wealth in water brands isn't universal throughout the world. While there have been incredible strides toward eliminating the global water crisis, data collected in 2023 by the World Health Organization and UNICEF revealed that there are still over 700 million people on earth without access to minimally clean water sources. There remains a desperate need for clean, accessible water throughout the world.

A number of years ago, I got to witness this problem firsthand when my church's young adult ministry traveled to Central America on a ministry trip. While we were involved in various activities, our primary goal was to assist our partners in drilling and establishing a local water well in a rural community that had little to no access to sustainable, clean water.

If you've ever been part of a water-drilling endeavor, you know it is messy business. The rig is a sight to behold. It's a massive piece of machinery that, when used correctly, does most of the work for you. Our task as volunteers was to divert the surfacing water away from the drilling sight by digging trenches, canals, and pockets to store the excessive water. The objective was to keep the dig sight as visible and clear as possible. It quickly became an I'll-never-be-able-to-use-these-jeans-again type of job. We looked like five-year-old kids who couldn't resist the temptation of some post-storm, puddle stomping. Eventually, you just embrace the mud and the mess.

We were there for several days, testing our water-traffic control abilities while the trained professionals operated the rig. The days were long, and that Central American heat was no joke. An air of anticipation loomed over us as we waited to know whether our work would be in vain. In a rural community like the one we found ourselves in, there is a real risk of drilling in a location that doesn't hold a long-term, sustainable water source. As the days went by, our partners grew more and more convinced that our drilling sight held real promise. Eventually, we heard the words we had all hoped for: "We've drilled far enough; this spot will work."

Relieved at the good news, we were all excited about the endeavor's success. We had found water, apparently enough to sustain the community for quite some time. There was just one problem. The job wasn't finished. Finding the water wasn't our goal—it was merely the first step. Establishing a system by which people could access the water was the goal. Once we found it, we had to implement the necessary equipment to make the water accessible and drinkable.

You see, had we gone all that way, spent all that money, worked all those days just to discover where water was, we would have wasted our time. Our goal was not simply to prove where the water was but to bring the water out. A sustainable source of water is worthless unless it's accessible. There had to be a means by which the water could be sustainably extracted. The location of the water, while important, is irrelevant if you don't have the means to access it. Thankfully, we were able to get everything set up, see that the newly dug well was consistently producing water, and hand over responsibility of the well to a local church in the community. But that happened only after we made a means to draw out the water that had always been there.

Time to Grab the Pail

We've reached a similar place in our study. We've established where to find satisfaction and why it's a trustworthy source, but this discovery serves as our starting line, not our finish line. It's not all that helpful to divulge where satisfaction can be found without offering a means to access it. There is a world of difference between professing that Jesus offers satisfaction and actually being satisfied in Him.

If we are honest, satisfaction is a lot easier to affirm theologically than it is to apply practically. We know that saying Christ satisfies is something Christians agree on. It's what all "good Christians" say, right? But it becomes a much more difficult confession when we are scrolling through other people's seemingly perfect lives on Instagram or find ourselves spending another Friday night alone. In those moments when an overwhelming feeling of insignificance and loneliness sneaks into our soul, satisfaction seems to retreat from the tip of our tongue and the scope of our perspective.

We need more than the often-discouraging conviction that we *should* be satisfied in Him. We need to know how to find and live in the satisfaction He offers. So having identified the true and trustworthy source of satisfaction, let's consider by what means we can draw it out and drink it for ourselves.

1. The Foundation of Knowing Him Intimately

While it may go without saying, knowing Jesus intimately is too important to leave out. If you are going to find satisfaction in Christ, you must begin by having a personal relationship with Him. We spent all of Chapter Three discussing who God is in an objective and theological sense. While this is certainly beneficial knowledge, it is useless to our lives unless we personalize it. It's not enough to know things about God generally; life only comes through knowing Him personally.

Most people live with a superficially pleasing view of humanity's relationship with the Divine. We hear things such as "we are all God's children" or "the Big Man in the sky is looking after all of us." On the surface, these sound appealing and uniting—perhaps even utopian. But these concepts fall shamefully short of the truth.

As we've already discussed throughout our study, sin has eternally separated us from God and has disrupted any sort of personal intimacy we had with Him. So while God is each and every person's Creator, not everyone is His child. And while He is certainly sovereign over everything, He is not everyone's Shepherd. Knowing God in such a personal way can only come through faith in Jesus. This is exactly what Jesus meant when He said, "I am the way, the truth, and the life. No one comes to the Father except through Me" (John 14:6). He was stating that He alone can provide the means to restore the severed relationship between humanity and God.

That is where satisfaction begins. If Jesus is the source of satisfaction and fulfillment in life, how can we ever expect to experience those things if we don't know Him? As C. S. Lewis once wrote, "God cannot give us a happiness and peace apart from Himself, because it is not there. There is no such thing." While our notion of satisfaction expands beyond just peace and happiness, Lewis' thought remains relative and needed. Satisfaction cannot be had apart from God because it doesn't exist apart from Him. Only when we enter into a relationship with the Father through the Son can we begin to experience the fullness of life we crave.

2. The Necessity of Abiding in Him Incessantly

If knowing God intimately makes satisfaction possible, then abiding in Him incessantly is what makes satisfaction accessible.

Though the word *abide* isn't common in modern vernacular, it is an important biblical concept and a vital aspect of satisfaction. The word carries various nuances and connotations, yet the simplest definitions of *abiding* should revolve around the notion of remaining or continuing in a place.

In our fast-paced society, abiding has become a lost art. Our days are often dominated by demanding schedules of jumping from place to place, class to class, and shift to shift with very little time for anything else. We are so used to being on the go that sitting still has become uncomfortable. If abiding sounds synonymous with boredom or waste, I get it. But when we talk about abiding in Christ, it's neither boring nor wasteful. It's actually our source of life, passion, and direction.

The most popular biblical instruction of abiding comes from Jesus's teaching in John 15. In that passage, Jesus is only a handful of hours away from His arrest, trial, and crucifixion. He is sharing one final meal with His closest friends and most intimate disciples. The instruction to abide comes in the middle of an ongoing illustration Jesus is using about branches, vines, and gardeners. Ultimately, the point Jesus is trying to make with His disciples revolves around spiritual fruitfulness. Jesus says:

> *Abide in Me, and I in you. As the branch cannot bear fruit of itself, unless it abides in the vine, neither can you, unless you abide in Me. I am the vine, you are the branches. He who abides in Me, and I in him, bears much fruit; for without Me you can do nothing.*
>
> —John 15:4–5

The point is clear. Unless the disciples learn to abide in Jesus, they will never produce spiritual fruit, as all good branches are expected to do. They must remain, or continue, in Christ if they are to produce spiritual fruit.

What is the spiritual fruit Jesus is talking about? It likely alludes to a few things, including the multiplication of Christians through the means of evangelism and discipleship. However, the primary idea behind spiritual fruit refers to the qualities of character in our lives that come as the result of being both with and like Jesus. It's what the Apostle Paul calls "the fruit of the Spirit." In Galatians 5:22–23, Paul declares that the fruit of the Spirit are the characteristics of love, peace, longsuffering (patience), kindness, goodness, faithfulness, gentleness, and self-control. These characteristics are manifested in the Christian life as a person draws near and continues in community with the Holy Spirit.

Consider the relevance of this teaching in light of our discussion about satisfaction. While the fruit of abiding isn't exactly at the top of the qualifications list for your local fraternity—as in not many young adults are very interested in godly living—it's in these fruits that we begin to glimpse what satisfaction in life can look like. I mean, who doesn't want a life filled with love, peace, patience, kindness, goodness, faithfulness, gentleness, and self-control? We spend lifetimes trying to earn these things in various ways. That is why Jesus's instruction is so vital.

If these fruits are to be ours, it will only be through constant continuance in the vine, which sources these characteristics. Once again, the words of C. S. Lewis prove helpful. He said, "If you want to get warm you must stand near the fire: if you want to be wet you must get into the water. If you want joy, power, peace, eternal life, you must get close to, or even into, the thing that has them." This is exactly the feat that abiding performs. It grants us constant exposure to the source of satisfaction and continual cultivation of being made like Jesus.

This begs the question: What does it look like to abide in Christ? The answer has been the subject of countless books and sermons over the last two millennia. While we don't have the space to elaborate here, if we were to take the time to work through the whole discourse of John 15, we'd find that Jesus gives us the answer alongside the instruction. To abide in Christ means to stay near or remain in His presence, His purposes for us, His purging of us, His precepts to us, His pleasure for us, and His positioning of us (John 15:1–15).

Practically speaking, abiding directly correlates to our personal spiritual disciplines. Specifically, we surround ourselves with Christ through the means of prayer, Scripture reading, and gathering together with His people for worship, study, and accountability. That means if you are failing to participate in these activities in your life there is a 100 percent chance you are failing to abide in Him. And I guarantee that when you fail to abide in Him, you will struggle to be satisfied in Him. So for the sake of fullness in life, never stop drawing near to Jesus. Begin by building daily habits of hearing Him through His Word, communing with Him through prayer, and worshiping Him through moment-by-moment surrender.

3. The Discipline of Delighting in Him Intentionally

The last means of drawing satisfaction comes in a much less obvious form. If you have spent even a minimal amount of time in church, my first two suggestions of knowing Him and abiding in Him probably came as no surprise. However, there remains another important step in finding satisfaction in Christ that often flies under the radar. It is the intentional discipline of finding our delight in the Lord.

When you hear the word *delight*, what comes to mind? For some reason, my mind replays the joyful, contented sigh Buddy the Elf makes when he bites (or inhales) his pop-tart-crusted, maple-syrup-drenched, spaghetti. He is delighting in his concoction. Perhaps more relatable is the first bite of a decadent dessert around the holidays or the first sip of a well-crafted latte. Either way, the imagery gets the point across. To delight in something is to find deep, sincere, fulfilled pleasure or enjoyment in that object.

Do you know that the Bible actually instructs us to delight ourselves in the Lord? In Psalm 37:4, King David poetically writes, "Delight yourself also in the LORD, and He shall give you the desires of your heart." While the verbiage is slightly debated, the implication of the verse is largely agreed on. Believers are to intentionally place their delight in the Lord. As a result, we are told that the desires of our heart will be given to us.

Let me first point out the subtle inference David makes in the verse regarding the nature of this delight. According to David, delight in the Lord is no accidental emotional state that we bump into one day; it's a discipline that we must intentionally decide to implement in our lives. That means no one is going to *make* you delight in God. Such forced delight, by definition, isn't authentic delight. Instead, we must choose to delight in Him.

Sometimes, this comes easily. Delighting isn't hard during the spiritual highs that accompany big events like walking across a stage for graduation, standing in a crowd of thousands at a Christian conference, or landing that second date after you thought you blew it on the first one. But here is the problem. True delight isn't contingent on momentary happiness or current circumstances. True delight is a choice we make to find joy in knowing Jesus regardless of what's happening in our life. It's a posture of our heart that we must choose moment by moment, day by day, in the highs and in the lows. It's when we walk across the stage for a diploma *and* when we bomb a final. It's when we stand in a crowd of thousands *and* when we are the only one who showed up to a Bible study. It's when we land that second date *and* when we get smacked with the "it's not you, it's me" breakup line. In each season, our hearts can be full of delight because of who He is to us and what He's done for us. Delighting is a willful discipline, not an emotional reaction.

As we delight in the Lord, He will give us the desires of our heart. Sounds good, right? If I just pay my dues, so to speak, and offer the Lord a bit of gratitude for His obvious blessings, He will give me whatever I want. Though it sounds like a promise of blessing and prosperity, the verse isn't saying that we will find ourselves in a Rolls Royce just because we walked into Sunday service with a smile on our face. The verse is actually promising something much greater.

The key to understanding the verse comes through emphasizing the delighting, *not* the consequential receiving. The delighting is what defines what we receive. If I could paraphrase the verse for the sake of simplification, here is what it would say: "God will satisfy your greatest desire when your greatest desire is God Himself."

While this may initially feel like a copout on the promise, it's not. It's a miracle. Sure, God may not be promising to be your personal genie, but He's actually promising something much better. He promises that when we delight in Him, when we seek Him and search after the satisfaction of knowing Him, He doesn't withhold Himself from us. To think that the God of the universe in all His majesty and might will willingly and unreservedly give Himself to us as we learn to desire Him is incomprehensible. That is the epitome of grace and generosity.

That means that those who delight in the Lord are never denied satisfaction. You see, satisfaction is not so much about learning to get what we want as it is about learning to want the right thing. When He becomes the prize we are seeking, we never have to worry about leaving empty-handed. He readily gives Himself to all sincere seekers of delight. The key is cultivating such delight in our own lives.

Delight can look like a lot of things once we apply it to our lives. David gives us multiple examples of delight, even within Psalm 37. Sometimes delight looks like trusting in God's justice (verses 1–2). Sometimes it's resting in and waiting on Him (verse 7). Ultimately, delighting is more about an attitude of the heart than it is an action of the body. Our actions will follow the direction of our delights.

So learn to delight in the Lord, even in the monotonous goings on of life. As you fight to abide through spiritual disciplines, delight in the Lord. As you wrestle with feelings of loneliness and insignificance, delight in the Lord. As you struggle for zeal and direction, delight in the Lord. As goes our delight, so goes our satisfaction.

Taste and See

I grew up in a sports household. While I can gratefully attest that sports didn't dominate our family priorities or schedule, they most certainly dominated our TV. Outside the obvious exceptions of *American Idol* auditions, a seasonal Christmas movie, or my dad's obligatory life lessons from *The Andy Griffith Show*, there was always a game on in the living room. That is why it came as a complete shock to me when my wife during our first year of marriage suggested we watch a holiday baking competition.

I admit that I was skeptical at first. The fact that an entire Food Network existed was news to me. But nonetheless, we started watching a show called *Holiday Baking Championship,* and I was hooked. Watching people create these incredible-looking Halloween or Christmas desserts was oddly entertaining. And that show was just the start. Soon, I found myself hooked on the hard stuff—*The Great British Baking Show*. It may have been the British accents, but I found the show enjoyable even if it was just background noise while I scrolled on my phone or took a nap.

However, despite my newfound interest in baking shows, there was one insurmountable problem. They are an inhumane form of torture. They may be filled with smiling faces, kind gestures, and warm pastries, but don't let that fool you. They cross a line on irreverence for human benevolence and should be outlawed internationally. Alright, maybe I'm overreacting.

But they are still torturous! They expect me to sit and watch bakers create the most elaborate desserts for hours on end yet never give me a chance to taste it for myself. Granted, until Willy Wonka's chocolate-delivering TV technology is realized, it remains impossible to eat what we see on the screen. But knowing this impossibility doesn't make me any less hungry while I'm watching. I still find myself wanting to taste what they just baked. Unfortunately, baking shows will always demand that viewers be spectators and not test-tasting participators.

Here's the good news. Jesus isn't a baking show. Satisfaction in Christ isn't a spectator-only sport. The invitation of Christ is not to sit back and never touch; it's the very opposite. David pleads with his readers in Psalm 34:8 to "taste and see that the Lord *is* good." Don't just theoretically believe that God is good. Experience it for yourself.

This is the invitation of Christ. You don't have to simply affirm with your mind that Christ satisfies; you can experience His satisfaction in a personal, authentic way. So learn to know Him intimately, to abide in Him incessantly, and to delight in Him intentionally.

part three

THE SIGNS OF SATISFACTION

The woman then left her waterpot, went her way into the city, and said to the men, "Come, see a Man."
—John 4:29–30

~ *chapter five* ~
POSTURES OF THE HEART

In high school, my friends and I were extremely talented at finding ridiculous things to pass the time during our slower classes. I guess when you're stuck with the same group of people eight hours a day for most of the year, your desperation for entertainment offers good camaraderie. For example, we found it entertaining to pretend to be an impromptu drum line. All it took was for one guy to start tapping his pen. Then one by one, everyone joined in with a different sound or rhythm until it sounded like those cringy, camp-rock-esque song outbreaks. Don't judge us; we were the *High School Musical* generation. (Okay, so maybe judge us.)

There was also the short span of time when paper football became our reason for existing. We would rush through our work each period in order to return to what "really mattered." We had some extremely intense tournaments with very tedious rules. While I can't say I learned Spanish, I did develop a pretty decent paper football field goal kick that admittedly has failed to help me in adulthood—yet. I think that day is still coming.

Of all the things we did to pass time, there was a solid six-month span when all we did was play card games. While the games would sometimes vary, there was one game that became a favorite. We called it Cash. You may be familiar with this game; most people call it Kemps. The game is simple. There are four players divided into two teams. Each player, having four cards in their hand, is tasked with acquiring four of a kind of their own choosing. The first player to acquire four of a kind wins. The trick is that a player is not allowed to declare that they have completed the task. Instead, their teammate must declare it for them by shouting "cash!" on their behalf. The only way to communicate with your teammate is through a secret sign that you predetermine before the game.

The sign for victory could be anything. The more subtle it is, the better. It could be something as simple as changing the way you hold your cards, motioning a certain way with your finger, or putting your elbows on the table. If the other team intercepts the sign, they can call "cash" first and steal the victory. Not only do you have to worry about getting the right cards in a relatively fast-paced game, but you also have to be looking for your partner's signal.

My tactic while playing was simple. I was the boy who cried wolf. I would subtly yet clearly try to give fake signs throughout the game. If I could convince the other team to yell "cash" before I was ready, they'd lose. So I'd do all sorts of stuff to try to confuse and deceive.

I knew that because the other team didn't know the sign, they could easily mistake a fake sign for the real thing. Only my partner could correctly distinguish between the fake signs and the real one. Knowing this filled me with the confidence to throw out all sorts of fake signs without fear of confusing my partner. Why? Because I trusted that my partner knew which sign to look for. While our opponents were busy trying to decipher all the other signs, my teammate could patiently ignore everything until the real one came up. Knowing what to look for makes all the difference.

Knowing What to Look For

When it comes to satisfaction, I've found that a large part of our frustration comes from being confused about what to look for. The problem isn't that satisfaction exists as an obscure, unidentifiable notion; rather, the problem is that most people have no idea what real satisfaction looks like. Make no mistake about it, when someone is truly, deeply, and biblically satisfied in life, it will be evidenced in their life. We've already been hinting at some of the evidence throughout this study. There are clear and obvious signs of satisfaction, yet most people are falling for the fake signs.

It's so easy to look around and mistake what we see in other people's lives as satisfaction. We see the influencer who has half a million followers, and by comparison, we feel unsuccessful. We see that one couple constantly post the most cliché date night photos, and by comparison, we feel unloved and unwanted. We see our high school friends getting their degrees and prestigious job offers, and by comparison, we feel insignificant for lacking personal direction. We see wealthy people driving cars that cost more than we earn in a year, and by comparison, we feel financially broke. We see these signs and assume their life is better or more satisfying than ours. What we fail to realize is that followers don't equal success, dates don't equal love, degrees don't equal significance, and riches don't equal happiness.

We are convinced that our lives are incomplete and dissatisfying because we are looking for the wrong signs. And if we are to ever find liberation from our comparisons and the freedom to live satisfied in Christ, we must learn what satisfied living really looks like. This begs the question: What does a satisfied life look like?

We've already gotten a few hints from King David in Psalm 23 and from the Apostle Paul in Galatians 5:22–23. While we can't exhaust the extensive list of ways Jesus's satisfaction is evidenced in our life, we can highlight a few of the major ones. To do this, we need to consider how satisfaction impacts two particular areas of lives—the postures of our heart and the patterns of our behavior.

Postures of the Heart

When it comes to evidence of satisfied living, we must first look inside toward the postures of the heart. That is primarily because the gospel we have been talking about transforms us from the inside out. That is Jesus's standard operation procedure. As with every aspect of redemption, the first fruits of satisfaction are deep within our hearts and work outward to our actions. As you well know, we can easily modify our behavior for any number of reasons. People can *act* like they are satisfied all day long.

But our actions, though important, are empty without a sincere change of heart. So in looking for satisfaction, we must work outward from the heart.

You may be wondering what a posture of the heart is. It's a churchy phrase that sounds fancy but simply refers to the inner attitudes and characteristics of our soul—the positioning of our hearts toward God in our life. In application, heart posture is the mindset by which we interpret, assess, and respond to the events and circumstances in our life. And when our heart is truly and deeply satisfied in Christ, it shows in our heart and attitude in a number of ways.

Extensive Contentment

Contentment isn't a particularly praised or celebrated concept in our society. We are the overnight-delivery generation. What we covet today can be on our porch tomorrow morning. We are accustomed to wanting more and getting it quickly. While contentment may be a nice concept from yesteryear, it's culturally common to subtly ask what place it really holds in our world today.

Though it may be popularly labeled a disposable, vintage virtue, contentment actually rests firmly at the center of and holds an important key for our conversation in satisfaction. In fact, the word *contentment* is a synonym for the word *satisfaction*, especially within the biblical context. According to the *International Standard Bible Encyclopedia*, contentment means "to be free from care because of satisfaction with what is already one's own." That is, when we are satisfied with what we already have, we will be free from the need to constantly pursue more.

Few biblical examples better demonstrate contentment than what the Apostle Paul wrote in Philippians.

> *I have learned in whatever state I am, to be content: I know how to be abased, and I know how to abound. Everywhere and in all things I have learned both to be full and to be hungry, both to abound and to suffer need. I can do all things through Christ who strengthens me.*
> —Phil. 4:11–13

As cool as it looked on Tim Tebow's eye-black, these verses have nothing to do with a person's physical ability to win championships. It has everything to do with enduring life's toughest losses. It is Paul's confession that because of Christ and the sustaining strength He gives, no circumstance or material context can rob him of satisfaction. In feast or in famine, in bounty or in need, Paul does not need to pursue anything more than Christ's sustaining and satisfying strength. It is a physical contentment born from spiritual satisfaction in Christ.

That particular correlation is important. Both in Paul's example and in our established biblical definition, contentment means to be "carefree" *because* of satisfaction; that is, it is the result of being satisfied. That is why it is the prime sign to look for in satisfaction assessments, regardless of how uncomfortable it might be.

For just a moment, let's agree to be as brave and transparent as we can with our own hearts. Answer this question honestly: Are you so satisfied in knowing, abiding, and delighting in Christ that if your life—as it is right now in this moment— never changed, you would be okay? I don't mean "okay" as mere survival or minimal existence. I'm asking about vitality, joy, and liveliness. If you never get your dream job, if you never receive what you are praying for, if your longed-for wedding day never comes, if you never have children, if you end up spending the next 50 years working the same job in the same city around the same people, is Jesus enough for you to be satisfied? Would you be satisfied in the right now even if the right now is all there will be?

I know that's not a comfortable thought for most people. We all have things we are hoping, praying, and waiting for. We all have certain ambitions or desires for our future, especially during young adulthood and the college years. I'm not suggesting you shouldn't want these things. It's natural and good to desire career advancement, marital relationships, or a change of circumstantial scenery. But if they don't come, do you have a contentment-giving satisfaction in Christ?

How you answer that question reveals a lot about your definition of and discipline in satisfaction. The simple truth is that if you are waiting for any sort of external circumstance to bring you some notion of completion or satisfaction, you are still trying to draw from an empty well. Even good things like marriage, promotions, and adult independence will leave you wanting when you expect too much from them. They over-promise and under-deliver when they become the attempted source of our satisfaction. And while they are good things worth pursuing, any joys they bring are shallow streams that flow from God's abounding ocean of goodness, never the other way around.

In this is the secret of contentment—knowing that God's goodness is always responsible for life's blessings yet never jeopardized in life's frustrations. God is good regardless of what's happening in life. His goodness in your life may not look like a six-figure job or a marriage license, but it's nonetheless present in countless other ways. Being content with what He gives and not obsessed with what He hasn't is a clear sign that satisfaction in Christ is present in our hearts.

Explicit Joyfulness

Depending on which version of the Bible you are studying, the word joy appears around 200 times. Though popularly associated with happiness, the biblical notion of joy runs much deeper than a temporal or reactionary feeling rooted in pleasant circumstances. While it is deeply tied to an emotional and mental state of being, Scripture speaks of joy as something we are to actively choose, even when life seems to give us little reason to be happy.

Take a longer look at the book of Philippians, and you will see that it's not just a prime example of contentment; it's even more so an authoritative appeal to joy. Paul references joy 16 times in just 104 verses. Joy is the obvious theme and faithful thread throughout the entire letter, which is surprising since Paul wrote it when he was in prison.

There is no room for debate on what is going on in Paul's mind and heart. He is so deeply joyful despite his circumstances that nearly every page of the letter is dripping with his satisfaction in Christ. In the first chapter, he is joyful knowing that his suffering is leading to gospel proclamation. In the second chapter, he is joyful in the unity of the church body who, when living in humility, look like their Savior before whom they will soon stand. In chapter three, he is joyful even while counting everything as loss for the incomparable satisfaction of knowing and walking with Jesus. In chapter four he is joyful in the satisfying provision of the Lord and fellowship of the body of Christ. Over and over and over again, Paul's joy seems to overflow from his transcendent satisfaction in who Christ is and what Christ is doing despite Paul's present trial. Even the "I can do all things" verse that we looked at in the previous section was pillared by Paul's joyfulness.

We could spend hours dissecting and applying Paul's joyfulness in Philippians. We could spend many additional hours observing and elaborating on the satisfied joy on display in the lives of many other biblical characters. There's truly no shortage. And that is exactly my point. The Scripture is clear. Those most deeply satisfied in Christ were also those most visibly joyful in life. It's almost as if joyfulness were the standard of life in Christ, like it is some obvious result of being at peace with God and living within His purposes. Maybe—just maybe—that's because it is. The goodness of the gospel, the grandeur of God, and the fulfillment of knowing Jesus is too weighty to not impact our emotional disposition. How could we possibly make such ginormous claims and *not* be joyful?

This isn't to insinuate that every moment of your life will be happy or easy. Joy in Christ doesn't always look like smiley-faced worship. Sometimes joy looks like weeping through sorrow with an emotional heart that clings to hope in the midst of hurt. Sometimes joy looks like trusting that Jesus is good when life is not. Sometimes joy looks like resting in the promise of new life while we wrestle with the fallout of the present one. Joy doesn't always wear a smile, but it is still always joy.

Joy doesn't waver or wane. It finds goodness in the simplicity of walking with Jesus each day. It knows nothing of drudgery. It transforms duty and obligation to eagerness and zeal. It doesn't sigh at the repetitive disciplines of walking with Christ but leans in and finds the life they offer.

Do you know this joy—a joy so deeply rooted in the satisfaction of life with Christ that even the grimmest of circumstances fail to defeat you? Or is your emotional disposition equivalent to waves in the sea, tossed back and forth with every turn of the wind? Are your emotions so rooted in your circumstances that you are guilty of forgetting how good Jesus is when life isn't? Does following Jesus feel like an obligation to you? Are you keeping a list of rules, fighting uphill for motivation to do religious chores, and begrudgingly maintaining religious habits for the sake of keeping up appearances or avoiding internal guilt? Such attitudes are the enemies of satisfaction. They teach us that Jesus is burdensome, wearisome, or secondary. Your emotional disposition speaks volumes about your state of satisfaction.

But if anyone on planet earth has reason to rejoice, is it not us, we who have been reconciled to God through the finished work of Jesus? Is it not we who have been made sons and daughters, co-heirs, co-laborers, and partakers of the Kingdom? Is it not we who have been restored to the very purpose of our design, who have been entrusted with the living water that springs up into eternal life? If such news cannot fill us with satisfaction and obvious joy, then I'm sure there is nothing on earth that can.

Eternal Anticipation

To date, the most watched movie trailer of all time belongs to Marvel's *Deadpool and Wolverine* with a total of 365 million views online within 24 hours of its initial release. That means in one day it had more views than America has citizens. But it's hardly surprising, considering how dominant Marvel Studios has been over the last two decades. In fact, six of the ten most watched trailers of all time are Marvel movies.

Could you imagine if absolutely no one went to see one of these movies, even after the movie trailer dominated online and created an enormous amount of buzz? We would assume that either the trailer did a horrible job of selling the story or the story wasn't worth watching. But what if hypothetically it wasn't either of those things? What if the trailer was so good that people were content just watching it over and over? Imagine if they still talked like they'd seen the movie and behaved as if they had. They bought the T-shirts, collected the souvenir popcorn buckets, and probably dominated an online chat club. Imagine they convincingly pose as raging fans for a movie they've only seen the trailer for.

At a minimum, we'd pity this type of confusion. More likely, we'd call out their hypocrisy or simply consider them crazy. We know that as exciting as a movie trailer may be, it is only designed to make you want more of the movie. A trailer may consist of clips from the movie, but it cannot truly compare to the entire film. It's a foretaste intended to hold just enough exciting satisfaction to make you crave the bigger thing. It would be a complete contradiction to claim you love something you don't want more of. You may be able to judge a movie by its trailer, but you can't truly love a movie by its trailer. We measure satisfaction in the trailer not by how diligently someone rewatches the same three-minute clip but by how they crave the actual movie.

In a very similar way, this present life in Christ is the trailer, and heaven is the full movie. While only Christ can offer true satisfaction in this life, it's a satisfaction that is never fully realized until the next. We are only getting a preview, a foretaste. Don't get me wrong. There is a fullness of life to be had now, but this present fullness pales compared to the fullness of life that awaits us in heaven. That's not because our present satisfaction is fake or cheap but because it's handicapped by a world of sin and brokenness. The gift is good, but the poor context weakens the taste.

I know that sounds like a complete contradiction. If satisfaction means to be filled and full, how can we be filled and still long for more? Isn't longing proof of dissatisfaction? How can satisfaction in Christ be described as both "now" and "not yet"?

This is the great paradox of the gospel message. Jesus has ushered in the Kingdom of God, yet we still await the day when it comes into its fullness. That doesn't mean His Kingdom hasn't been established. He has first established it in our hearts. But this very real, present reality, like any good movie trailer, is a legitimate but mere preview of the greater satisfaction to come. We are caught in a tension between the goodness of what God has already done in our hearts and the promise of an even more expansive goodness that He will fully realize for all creation in the days to come. It's a tension between rejoicing in what is and longing for what will be.

It's this very tension that rests at the center of the Christian heart and satisfaction. It's a logical necessity of the truth we've already given witness to in prior chapters, namely that Jesus alone is the source of satisfaction and that it's only in intimacy with Him that we can ever truly be satisfied. Should these two statements be true, there is only one reasonable response—a longing to be with Him. If it is true that in His presence is fullness of joy (Ps. 16:11), then where else could we possibly want to be but in His presence?

We were designed with desires and longings that will only be satisfied in Christ's physical and eternal presence. Once again, our obviously favorite guide through this satisfaction journey, C. S. Lewis, has something to add to the conversation. He famously said, "If I find in myself a desire which no experience in this world can satisfy, the most probable explanation is that I was made for another world." Though it sounds fantastical, it's true. You were made for another world—a world without sin, pain, or shame and a world where your satisfaction is complete in the God who designed you for His glory. So don't be surprised or frustrated when nothing in this world seems to do the trick. Anything and everything that does not last *cannot* fill.

That is why Paul urges Christians to "set your mind on things above, not on things on the earth. For you died, and your life is hidden with Christ in God. When Christ *who is* our life appears, then you also will appear with Him in glory" (Col. 3:2–4). Any claim we have to life cannot be disassociated from the One in whom our life consists. He is the source of our life, the security in our life, the advocate for our life, the procurer of our life. He is our life! That means we are only as alive as we are near Him. That is why Paul implores us to set our minds and our affections on heaven because that is where our life is found.

It's simple. If in His presence is the fullest of joys, the truest of satisfactions, and the very fulfillment of our created intent, then every day we go without Him will produce only ache and longing. It's not that we can't draw near to Him now; it's that our drawing near is veiled until the day we see Him face to face. While we have been incalculably blessed to have the means of prayer, corporate worship, and Scripture to draw near to Him in spirit, these are the tools of a long-distance relationship. They are intended to sustain us until the day we no longer need them. It will be a day when we need not cling to printed paper and bound leather because we are face to face with the Word Himself. It will be a day when we need not pray in faith because we will speak plainly in His presence. It will be a day when we need not gather as sojourners to worship a coming King because the King will have come and made all things new. And while we cherish these means of our present spiritual abiding, we know that He is the treasure to which they lead and the prize for which they instill longing.

Herein lies another test of our satisfaction. Is heaven on your heart? Do you find in your heart and soul an eager anticipation of Jesus's return and reign? Tasting His redemption in our hearts will, by default, produce an insatiable ache for the day when He doesn't just reign in our hearts but in all areas of our universe. In sampling His justice, we will long for His Kingdom. In sampling His peace, we will long for His throne. In sampling His grace, we will long for His glory. In sampling His glory, we will long for His praise. In sampling His satisfaction, we will long for His presence.

Satisfaction in Christ's person is saturated with great anticipation for Christ's return. What shallow affection it must be to claim a love that produces no longing, to lay claim to a satisfaction void of any desire for proximity. So set your heart and mind on things above. Live ruined for eternal things, recognizing that nothing on this side of heaven can compare to what awaits you on the other side.

Simple but Sure

In case you aren't picking up on what's unfolding, let me address the elephant in the chapter. Nothing of what we just covered is particularly innovative or revolutionary. The concept of contentment, of joyfulness, and of anticipation have been threaded into the very fabric of Christian living since the conception of the church. So if these concepts feel like basic Christianity, it's because they are.

But at what point did we become convinced that novelty determines relevancy? A simple truth isn't less true because it's simple. And the simplicity of biblical truth doesn't negate its importance or render it powerless. Could it be that many of us lack the simple satisfaction of following Jesus because we are looking for some new way to do it? What if the life we have been longing for has been staring at us this whole time, but we were too dismissive of its simplicity to see it?

These postures of the heart may be simple, but they are sure. Any heart that knows them well is sure to be satisfied. And any heart that knows them not is sure to still be wandering among empty wells.

~ *chapter six* ~
PATTERNS OF BEHAVIOR

What's the craziest thing you've ever done to convince someone you were telling the truth? Whatever your answer is, it's probably not as wild as the story of Richard Davis. In the late sixties, Davis was working as a pizza delivery man in Detroit, Michigan. One night on the job, he was ambushed and attacked by three armed robbers (as in, three men who had guns, not a group of criminals each possessing an extra physical arm; that would be a totally different story). While Davis, being armed himself, was able to shoot his way out of danger, the severity of the exchange revealed to him a great need in the modern world: the need for a bulletproof vest. There have, of course, been all sorts of attempts at body armor throughout the centuries. But most weren't truly bulletproof, and, if they were, they certainly weren't convenient enough to wear in a fight. Experiencing this need firsthand, Davis sought to invent a modern bulletproof vest of soft armor that was agile and lightweight.

After working tirelessly to perfect his product, Davis began marketing it to police departments and other emergency personnel. He arranged for various demonstrations of the vest's efficiency and durability.

Though impressive, watching a vest protect a watermelon or absorb a bullet on the ground didn't necessarily carry the same weight as if it had legitimately saved someone's life. So, Davis had to demonstrate his technology could, in fact, save a life. But how can you prove this without jeopardizing someone's life? Simply put, you can't! And, unsurprisingly, this wasn't the kind of experiment people lined up to be the guinea pig for. I mean, just imagine that help wanted sign!

Richard Davis was left with only one real option: become the guinea pig himself. If he was going to win the confidence of his potential customers and secure his lifesaving vest a spot in the body armor hall of fame, he had to prove it was able to do what he said it could do. With a video camera rolling and a handful of people watching, Davis nervously placed the thin white vest over his chest. He then grabbed a .44 magnum revolver and turned it on himself at point-blank range. After a few distressing moments, he pulled the trigger. With a flash of light and dramatic flair, the truth had been revealed: the vest was undoubtedly able to save a life. Davis stood up and painfully threw the vest off, while clearly suffering no significant injury. Over the next few decades, Richard Davis would go on to prove his product by performing this stunt over 190 times! Which would explain why his bulletproof vest soon became an integral part of body armor uniforms across the globe.

Actions Speak Louder Than Words

Richard Davis is a prime example of the old adage that actions speak louder than words. No doubt you've heard the phrase in some form or fashion throughout your years. The phrase itself became popular during the Civil War as a constant refrain of President Abraham Lincoln during a time riddled with diplomatic smokescreens and deep discord. Yet the maxim seems to expand across historical eras with specific phrases surfacing as early as the 13th century and echoing allusions even farther back.

While the adage may feel used and worn, that's in part because of its accuracy. It's used often because it is extremely true in life. Your actions do speak louder than your words. Your beliefs, priorities, and characteristics are consistently displayed in your actions, not just conveniently sprinkled in your speech. That's why the great industrial giant Andrew Carnegie once said, "As I grow older, I pay less attention to what men say. I just watch what they do."

This is not to suggest that we shouldn't speak true words but rather that our actions are the measure by which our belief in those words is deemed true. If we claim something is true, our actions must correspond appropriately to that claim. If our actions do not correspond with our claims, then it's fair to assume that either our claims are false or we don't really believe them.

This same principle also applies to satisfaction in Christ. If you really want to know if you are living satisfied in Christ, look at your lifestyle and actions. Satisfaction doesn't manifest itself only in the secret impulses and postures of our hearts. While it fundamentally must start there, it just as critically must work itself out in our behavior and action. Our actions and behavior may not be the basis for our faith, but they certainly serve as the fruit of it. To steal some genius from the Apostle James, show me your satisfaction *without* your works, and I'll show you mine *by* my works (see James 2:18).

You can tirelessly confess that Christ brings satisfaction to your life, but unless you live satisfied in Christ, your confession is empty. That, of course, begs the question: What does satisfaction in Christ look like when it's lived out—not merely in the deeper recesses of our hearts but applied to our hands? While there are plenty of habits, actions, and behaviors that could qualify, we will focus on the three most prominent and non-negotiable.

Exclusive Adoration

You're more likely to use the word adore during your daily, traffic-laden performance of Harry Styles than you are in conversations about your faith—unless it's the month of December. Then every song you sing in church includes the word *adore*.

While the popular connotation of adoration has been swept away by romanticism, which is not entirely unfair or improper, the theological expression of the word runs much deeper. Adoration in a fuller sense goes beyond a love-life infatuation and carries tones of veneration, worship, deep affection, and responsive surrender. It means to be so captivated by personal affection that you cannot help but respond with expressions of devotion, loyalty, and even submission.

When you search the Scriptures, it is exactly that kind of affection and devotion you see exemplified throughout all redemptive history as people behold God's majesty and mercy. From Abraham's obedience on Mount Moriah to John's vision on the Island of Patmos, we see example after example of men and women who were so in awe of divine glory, so unsettled by divine grace, and so observant of divine goodness that they couldn't help but be overcome with adoration at their God on display.

One of the clearest examples of this soul-satisfied adoration comes from David's song as recorded in Psalm 63. Likely written at a time when he was solitarily in the wilderness of Judah, David writes a song expressing the depth of joy he has found in the Lord's fellowship. After expressing his desperate, deer-after-water longing for the Lord, he wrote this:

> *Because Your lovingkindness* is *better than life,*
> *My lips shall praise You.*
> *Thus I will bless You while I live;*
> *I will lift up my hands in Your name.*
> *My soul shall be satisfied as with marrow and fatness,*
> *And my mouth shall praise You with joyful lips.*
> —Ps. 63:3–5

Notice that even when stranded in the wilderness, David is compellingly captivated by the better-than-life lovingkindness of God. It is better than the water his parched mouth longs for, better than the feast his empty stomach roars for, and better than the clean wilderness air his lungs heave for. Better than life itself is the steadfast love of God that David has experienced so intimately. While he is unsure of his future physical survival, the satisfaction of his soul is steady. "My soul shall be satisfied as with marrow and fatness" (Ps. 63:5).

But it's not David's display of satisfaction I want to draw your attention to; it's what follows. After stating that God's love is better than life and after expressing the soul-satisfying feast David experiences of God's goodness, he declares, "And my mouth shall praise *You* with joyful lips" (Ps. 63:5). Because God has so deeply satisfied him, David cannot help but express praise and adoration. That satisfaction he felt in his soul worked its way up to his lips.

On the one hand, it was a momentary, emotional response. As he reflects on God's love, he cannot help but express adoration. But understand that it didn't end there. It may have involved emotion, but it far exceeded an emotional high. He declares that he is going to continue praising, throughout all his life. David's decision was a from-now-on type, not based on his physical context but motivated by an overflowing reflex from God's indisputable goodness. His heart was determined to adore God who had satisfied him so deeply.

You see, satisfaction begets adoration. What you trust in to fill you is what will eventually spill out of you. If Christ is your source of fulfillment and joy, He will inevitably become your inescapable refrain. The heart that is satisfied in Christ will be manifest in the mouth and an overall lifestyle that adores Him.

Exhaustive Obedience

When you are truly and deeply satisfied in your pursuit of Christ, not only will your mouth praise Him but your behavior will be marked by obedience to Him. You will live a life of obedience to His Word, of yielding to His Spirit, and of growing into His likeness. You will seek to follow His ways in all areas of your life. Satisfaction in who He is always overflows in the pursuit of what He commands. Practically speaking, satisfaction is a close synonym to submission.

Consider that disobedience and rebellion are, at their very core, the fruit of dissatisfaction. Think of it in light of the biblical narrative. When did sin come into the world, and what motivated it? We know Adam and Eve ate of the fruit because they were deceived. But while the deception of the serpent may have placed the fruit in their hand, it was their own dissatisfaction with God's designed order and God's already given explanation that ultimately led them to take the bite. They believed that God was holding out on them, that an exalted level of existence could be theirs should they choose to discard God's boundaries. The serpent convinced them that God's design was robbing them of something better. And so the seeds of discontentment, sown into a field of desire, gave birth to sin and rebellion. The severity of Adam and Eve's sin wasn't merely the act of eating; it was that in their eating, they rebelled against God's good design and protective boundaries in order to pursue something they thought would be more satisfying. Discontent with a garden of literal perfection, they rebelled in chase of their own exaltation. Rebellion is the fruit of dissatisfaction.

That conversely implies that satisfaction ought to lead to obedience. When we recognize that God's design *is* good, that the commands He issues are *for* our good, and that the boundaries He emplaces are to *protect* our good, what need have we to disobey? Disobedience would only be ruining what is good.

But Scripture doesn't just exemplify this truth in an antithetical way; it also demonstrates clearly what life-giving obedience is to the soul who knows the Lord. We see this specifically in King David in Psalm 17. Like most of David's songs, Psalm 17 is filled with emotional range and heartfelt pleas to the Lord. Contextually, the psalm is a prayer for physical deliverance. However, there seems to be a diligent undertone not just of temporary reprieve but of eternal salvation. He ends his prayer by making this powerful confession: "As for me, I will see Your face in righteousness; I shall be satisfied when I awake in Your likeness" (Ps. 17:15).

Notice the importance of the word *righteousness*. David is saying that because he has been striving for righteousness (that is, right-ness in living according to God's standard) and because he has sought to live innocently before God in a world of sin, he will see the Lord. He's not claiming to be completely innocent of breaking God's law. Rather he is demonstrating the difference in lifestyles between him and his enemies. While they live wickedly, ignorantly, and negligently of God's law, David seeks to obey. Because he serves a righteous God, he wants to be obedient in righteousness. This obedience and pursuit of righteousness results in intimacy with the God of *all* righteousness.

But pay attention to what he says at the end. "I shall be satisfied when I awake in Your likeness." While some interpret this to be a reference to waking up in the morning and visiting with the Lord through some sort of divine manifestation, I think the simple reading is more preferable. David seems to be speaking of the end of his life, much like he had just spoken of the end of the wicked man's life in verse 14. The wicked build a fortune to only leave it behind. David isn't seeking that which he will have to leave behind but that which he will awaken to find. And what happens when David awakens after death? He will find himself perfected into the image of God and fully satisfied in such perfection. While David may not have thoroughly understood the full eschatological impact of his words, they seem to be eschatological, nonetheless.

David was resolved to this: In a world of wickedness and disobedience, he would pursue obedience *to* the Lord and would place his hope in being made *like* the Lord. His satisfaction is not in riches, fame, posterity, or legacy. His satisfaction is rooted in his likeness to God, and his likeness to God consists of his obedience to God's ways. His desire for satisfaction cultivated a life of obedience to the only One who could truly satisfy.

Don't misunderstand me on this point. Neither David's prayer nor my plea is that we offer obedience as a means of being awarded satisfaction. Our obedience isn't the currency by which we purchase God's goodness in our life. God's goodness and grace are already ours in Christ—fully, deeply, finally. We live as those already filled, not those working for filling. Obedience is the behavioral overflow of inward satisfaction in who God is and in enjoying His God-ness over us.

While we don't obey to be rewarded with satisfaction, David does remind us that there is a correspondence between the level of our obedience and the level of our satisfaction. God has made you to be an image-bearer. He made you to reflect and glorify Him in your life. While sin has deeply marred this image, Jesus came to restore it. That is why Scripture speaks of our being conformed to the likeness of Christ as the primary end of our God-given destiny (Rom. 8:29). It is the end for which God has redeemed us.

That means you are only truly succeeding in life when you are growing into Christ's likeness. When you learn to walk like Him, to talk like Him, to love like Him, to yield like Him, to give like Him, to pray like Him, to rejoice like Him, and to live like Him. When you are fulfilling the purpose for which you have been originally made in creation and remade in the cross of Christ. It is that pursuit of being like Him that serves as both evidence of your growing satisfaction and the fullness of this satisfaction realized.

It's at this point that most people fall off the wagon. Satisfaction in Christ sounds good until now. Who doesn't want to be filled with His peace, grace, love, joy, and fulfillment? But recognizing that the satisfaction He gives comes with expected loyalties to His Kingdom and submission to His ways often changes things. Obedience, while always good, isn't always easy. It certainly isn't always pretty. In fact, it could be quite costly.

Obedience to Christ could create some of the hardest circumstances of your life. People might ridicule, reject, or persecute you. You may not be socially better off for it. Obedience to God may not get you promotions. It may not land you a spot in the fraternity. There may be times when obedience to God demands disobedience to a person or distancing yourself from friends. There may be parties you no longer attend, words you no longer speak, music you no longer sing, substances you no longer take, habits you are forced to break, and even sorrows you are forced to face. And beyond the social fallout, obedience flies in the very face of the independence and self-sufficiency that you and I have been taught to build our lives on. Obedience demands that we resign from the throne of our life and start taking orders from another King. Obedience isn't easy.

But it's this difficulty that makes our obedience so powerful and revealing. Should we deem any of these challenges not worth facing or any of these consequences not worth suffering, our true conviction is revealed.

We would be believing that something else is better than Jesus, allowing a rival for the title of ultimate satisfier in our hearts. You see, the value of an object isn't determined by how much we want it but by how much we'd give up to have it. So what are others to think if they hear us claim that Christ offers satisfaction, yet we simultaneously refuse to yield control of our lives and walk in His satisfying ways? They'd think exactly what they should, that either Christ is lying or we are.

Do you want to demonstrate your satisfaction in Christ? Then devote yourself to living life with Christ, yielding to His ways, submitted to His throne, And obedient to His Word.

Explosive Witness

I have two toddlers at home who do their very best at all times to make sure there is as little of our floor visible as possible. It doesn't matter how often we pick up the toys. They find the deepest joy not in playing with the toys but in seeing them sprawled across the floor. I guess they operate on the assumption that they are more likely to remember to play with a toy after their dad painfully grumbles through an array of syllables, hops around on one foot, and has a near-death experience from the sole of his foot being punctured by the sharpest side *of said toy.*

While messy floors are only one frustration of parenting, nothing compares to seeing the proud joy on my sons' faces when they accomplish some feat during playtime. Whether it's putting on some goofy pair of sunglasses, building a tower out of magnetic blocks (which have been the source of many of those near-death experiences), or making a shot on their mini basketball hoop, they love to show off their accomplishments. In fact, they are always so proud and overcome with joy from their successes that they won't let me *not* see it. It doesn't matter what I'm doing, they will call out for my attention repeatedly until I've seen their special trick.

Why is that? Why do kids demand attention for what is a relatively small accomplishment? For starters, there is certainly an important developmental aspect involved. They are looking for approval, affirmation, and applause, which we know are essential for their development of confidence and independence.

But I also think there is something more simple, perhaps even innocent, about their pleas for attention. They seem to assume that good things need to be known. If something is good, fun, joyful, or pleasing, they innately desire to show others that very thing. It makes inherent sense to them that good things need to be made known to others.

That's a simple principle that most people operate on throughout their life. When we were born, our parents announced it. When we graduate, we announce it. When we get engaged, we announce it. When we have kids, we announce it. Thanks to social media, we even announce things like our daily coffee run, vacations, concerts, cat videos, and anything else we think the world needs to know. We like to make good things known.

The truth is that sharing good news isn't just a commendable impulse of human nature, it's the very demand of such goodness. It's not that *the knowing* supplies the action its goodness but rather that by virtue of its being good, it must be known. It would still be good whether or not someone else saw it, but it's deserving of attention nonetheless. It's not that good news *should* be shared; it's that good news *must* be shared.

We started our study by looking at the testimony of a Samaritan woman in John 4. Having gone full circle, we now return to the end of her journey to find application for the end of ours. Remember that she had been offered a satisfied life, a well of living water, sourced from the supposed Messiah. She had deflected His claims. She had seemingly avoided His conversational gaze. She had even been blindsided by her romantic past being blasted by this wandering prophet. And what does she do with all this? She immediately tells others.

In John 4:28–32, we find the account of what happened after the Samaritan woman talked with Jesus. She ran back into the city, leaving her water jar behind, to tell people about her conversation. That is significant because, as we discussed previously, she was an outcast. The townspeople were the ones she was seemingly trying to avoid. Yet now she is running directly to them. And more so, she leaves her water vessel at the well. Getting water was the very reason she had gone there in the first place.

Her conversation with Jesus had been so monumental that she abandoned her chore, disavowed her social evasion, rushed to the center of the city, and began telling people about Jesus. It was incredibly obvious that her encounter with Jesus wasn't something she could keep to herself. She had heard something too good to not make it known.

She simply goes to town and begins telling people about her conversation and pleading with them to come and investigate for themselves. She didn't offer some lengthy sermon. She didn't give a robust apologetic. She hadn't even really experienced the fullness of Jesus's promise yet. She was no expert in theology or some trainee apostle of the coming Kingdom. She simply knew that the goodness she had found offered in Christ needed to be known. She knew that if what Jesus said were true, she wasn't the only one who needed to know it. What could satisfy her could also satisfy others.

And because of her witness, many from the town became followers of Jesus. At first, they were merely intrigued by her testimony. Yet soon they proved convinced in their own hearts. Jesus had used the most unlikely person in the most unlikely place to start a spiritual movement among a neglected people in desperate spiritual need. What started as a promise of satisfaction for one woman turned into a revival for a whole city because she had understood that the living water was too good to not share.

Such is the case for sincere satisfaction. Like any other good news, though much more so, it demands to be shared. I'd argue that the sincerity of our satisfaction can be measured by how much we share the secret of its source. Can we really profess to have found satisfaction, purpose, and fulfillment in life while not telling the world around us of its whereabouts? Either we are incredibly stingy or we haven't found what we claim to have found.

The simplest test of your satisfaction in Christ is your witness for Christ. Your longings aren't unique. The world around you is filled with real people who have real longings and real desires to know what they were made for. If you believe Jesus is who He says He is and will do what He's promised to do, you will share that with the people around you who desperately need hope. In fact, not sharing *might* be worse than not knowing it. It's certainly more selfish. The only thing more tragic than a lost soul is a silent Christian. There is true, satisfying life in knowing Jesus, and the people in your world need to know that.

What Do the Signs Say?

While what we've learned so far is by no means exhaustive, we have now shed some light on a few of the more major signs of our satisfaction. Between these postures of the heart and patterns of our behavior, we can reasonably and confidently begin to assess our own life through those lenses.

Maybe you've made it this far and now find yourself discouraged by the lack of correspondence between your life and these characteristics. Don't lose heart. These signs serve not only as convicting measures to reveal our present state but also as ideal measures for which we strive. If you are struggling with your contentment, your joyfulness, your heavenly anticipation, your obedience, your adoration, or your witness, don't run the other way in defeat. If the whole premise of our journey is that these characteristics are found in satisfying life with Christ, the absence of these traits ought to usher us only ever nearer to Him, not away from Him.

If the signs we've discussed are characteristics by which you long for your life to be defined, then take heart. They are readily available in Christ. If you want the signs of satisfaction, simply be sure to wander not far and linger not long from their source.

~ *conclusion* ~
NO OTHER STREAM

In the United States, every state requires all motor vehicles to have their registrations renewed every one to two years. In my home state of Texas, the law demands an annual renewal. But do you know that you *actually* have to do it?

For some reason, I operated for a long time on the theory that this law was more of a suggestion. However, the police officer who pulled me over for expired tags didn't agree with my interpretation of the law. Instead, I was awarded a fine for violating the standard for motor vehicle ownership in Texas.

For months I had told myself that it wasn't a big deal. I also told other people it wasn't a big deal. When approached by my own parents about renewing the sticker, I—in my independent, self-sufficient, young-adulthood glory—assured them that there was no need to panic. I mean, there were far worse things going on in my city. Why would the numbers on my car windshield take any sort of priority?

Plus, do you know what is involved in renewing your registration? I'd have to drive all the way to the DMV (a painstaking nine miles from my house), take a number, sit in a waiting room with dozens of other people, pay a processing fee, put a new sticker on my windshield, and—most difficult of all—manage to get the old sticker off my windshield. Was it worth it, considering that no one would probably ever notice?

As soon as I received the ticket, I had the answer to my question. It would have been worth it. Not a single part of the renewal process was all that difficult. It was inconvenient, but not difficult; I just so happen to share in the human tendency to confuse the two.

Worse than being confronted by my own laziness, I realized that a few months before I was pulled over, I had received a piece of paper in the mail telling me it was time to renew the registration. If I had taken the time to fill out this relatively short mailer, I could have gone to a number of local grocery stores and received my registration sticker from one of them. There would have been no driving the torturous nine miles, no waiting at the DMV, no sitting in a room with random people who all look equally frustrated and impatient. Of course, I'd still have to deal with the old sticker and all its frustrating residue, but some crosses we must always bear.

The sad reality is that I wasn't just presented with a standard to adhere to, but I was also given a gracious means to accomplish that standard with as much convenience as possible. Even though the state of Texas tried to make it easier for me, I failed to take advantage of it. And you know whose fault that was? Mine. Solely mine. Despite every attempt to get me to do what

I knew I needed to do, I ignored every caution, dismissed every suggestion, and avoided any accountability until it was too late.

In the end, I not only had to get the renewal but I also had to stop by the courthouse with proof of my renewal in order to avoid paying the fine. What I had initially done to avoid inconvenience ended up being even more time-consuming and inconvenient. Even worse, I had to confess to my parents that the police officer, for some strange reason, had agreed with their opinion about the sticker. My dad, being the gracious pastor that he is, responded with a smirk and an all-too-ready "I told you so." And truthfully, he had told me so. And so had the state of Texas. I just refused to listen.

Like a Horse and Its Water

Even if you've never heard the English proverb, "You can lead a horse to water, but you can't make it drink," you've at least now seen it exemplified. I was the horse, and my car registration renewal was the water. The proverb simply means that while you can do everything in your power to encourage someone to make the right or necessary decision, you cannot make that decision for them. You can control another person's willful behavior as much as you can force a horse to drink water. It may be exactly what the horse needs, but unless the horse recognizes that need and wants to satisfy it, it's more likely that you'll end up kicked than for the horse to end up drinking water.

Life has a way of letting us all play the stubborn horse at times. We fail to heed the warnings we hear. We fail to accept the advice we are given. We fail to sip from the stream that's been placed under our feet, even while dying of thirst. Often we are too lazy and too stubborn for our own good. We fail to do the right thing, even when it happens to be the easy thing.

Other times, we find ourselves playing the part not of the stubborn horse but of its patient guide. Have you ever pleaded with someone to make better decisions only to watch them intentionally and willfully walk the other way? You invest time, effort, and energy encouraging them to do the right thing, but they still end up choosing the wrong thing to their own detriment. It's a stinging pain. And it's one I've felt all too often in young adult ministry.

I have watched countless young adults dismiss the teachings of Scripture. I've looked into the faces of friends who tried to explain to me that they'd "give the Jesus thing a chance later on in life." I've watched as young adults convince themselves that they need to spend this season doing their own thing and would get serious about their faith when they were older. I've heard the excuses, provided the warnings, and watched the fallout that follows poor decisions. In truth, this book is such a warning and such a plea. It's my attempt to lead the horse to water. And I'm begging you to drink.

Things That Matter, Things That Don't

The pioneer missionary William Carey once said, "I am not afraid of failure; I'm afraid of succeeding at things that don't matter." While I've yet to meet someone who doesn't innately fear failure in some degree, I can't think of many who are scared of succeeding in the wrong things. In fact, I know people who intentionally set the bar too low in their life, thinking that minimized success is better than overly ambitious failure. But if the premise of this book is true—that Jesus alone satisfies our search, acts as our source, and produces in us the signs of true satisfaction—then the harsh reality is that most people are succeeding at things that don't really matter.

That might not be reflected in their bank accounts, the clothes they wear, the cars they drive, the titles they go by, the vacations they take, the houses they own, the status of their relationships, the people they sleep with, or the captions on their Instagram. By every observable appearance, they could be dripping of worldly success.

But what qualifies as success in this world doesn't necessarily correspond to success in the next. And what is material wealth truly worth when it's not the currency of heaven? What good is gaining the entire world yet losing your own soul? What good is the applause of people if your soul is not at peace with God? What is love from another person when your heart knows not the unsearchable love of Christ? What are any of these things apart from Christ? They are broken wells.

Broken wells may glisten from the morning dew, but confusing that dew as a faithful spring of water would be a fatal mistake. For as the sun rises higher, the dew evaporates by the heat, and anyone trusting it to quench their thirst will be left thirsty. Don't confuse the dew of worldly success as a spring from which to drink. When the Son returns, all that is not from Him, for Him, and to Him will surely be dispelled by His glory.

You don't have to spend your life succeeding in things that don't matter. You don't have to waste your life searching and overturning every glimmering stone. You don't have to attempt to discover yourself through soul-tossing social experimentation.

You don't have to sample at the world's table only to discover that the courses won't satisfy. You don't have to walk through the avoidable heartache of trusting in promises that were never capable of keeping their word. You don't have to deal with the consequential though sometimes seemingly delayed shame of forsaking the fountain (Jer. 17:13). You can determine today— even now— that you will only seek your satisfaction from Christ.

But What If You're Wrong?

My proposed resolution only makes sense if the claims in this book are true. Most of what I've written is theological, and some of what I've written is practical, but nothing I've written is hypothetical. It's either true or it's not. I don't claim it to be my truth. I don't present it as an option to be adopted as your truth. I claim it to be *the* truth. As with any truth claim, it's verifiable.

If any aspect of my plea sounds suspect, put it to the test. Do you question God's ability to supply satisfaction? Test it. Do you question the methods of accessing satisfaction? Test them. Are you skeptical of the signs of satisfaction? Try them. Put those things to the refiner's fire. Bend them to see if they break.

Foolishness is not a lack of suspicion but a lack of investigation. A person is no fool who shows suspicion to big claims. A person is a fool who can hear such claims and not investigate their validity. Nothing is to be lost in your trial, but if I am right, everything is to be lost in your passive dismissal. If I am wrong about satisfaction and its source or its signs, it's worth knowing, but even more so if I am right.

Make no mistake, you do not have to investigate. You don't have to lean into the biblical offer of living water. You can offer a variety of excuses for why I am mistaken. You can convince yourself that this message is for someone else. You can put this book down and go on living your life as if this book never existed. You can pass up this well in hopes of a deeper one to follow. But I must warn you that you'll be searching for a well that does not exist.

The Lion's Stream

In the sixth book of the beloved children's fantasy series *The Chronicles of Narnia*, a young boy named Eustace and a young girl named Jill find themselves transported to the magical world of Narnia. Although Eustace had been there once before with his cousins, Jill finds herself lost in a strange new world, weary and extremely parched.

Temporarily separated on their journey, Jill discovers a stream of flowing water, but only after a near encounter with a terrifying lion. The very sight and sound of the stream made her 10 times thirstier. But as she draws near the stream, she is distraught at the sight of the lion who has now made the bank of the stream its bed. In a way reminiscent of the Savior at a first-century Samaritan well, the Lion engages in conversation with the thirsty girl at the stream.

> "Are you not thirsty?" said the Lion.
>
> "I am dying of thirst," said Jill.
>
> "Then drink," said the Lion.
>
> "May I—could I—would you mind going away while I do?" said Jill.

The Lion answered this only by a look and a very low growl. And as Jill gazed at its motionless bulk, she realized that she might as well have asked the whole mountain to move aside for her convenience. The delicious rippling noise of the stream was driving her nearly frantic.

"Will you promise not to—do an thing to me, if I do come?" said Jill. "I make no promise," said the Lion.

Jill was so thirsty now that, without noticing it, she had come a step nearer. "Do you eat girls?" she said.

"I have swallowed up girls and boys, women and men, kings and emperors, cities and realms," said the Lion. It didn't say this as if it were boasting, nor as if it were sorry, nor as if it were angry. It just said it.

"I daren't come and drink," said Jill.

"Then you will die of thirst," said the Lion.

"Oh dear!" said Jill, coming another step nearer. "I suppose I must go and look for another stream then."

"There is no other stream," said the Lion.

Whether you are a fan of talking lions and magical lands or not, don't miss the parabolic significance of this. Jill had found the stream capable of satisfying every last ounce of her thirst, but in fear of the Lion, she hesitated. Could she trust the Lion not to hurt her? Should she expect him to move out of the way so the stream could be hers alone? What if her stooping to drink led to her demise?

For those familiar with Narnia, we know such questions are ridiculous. The Lion, that functions as the Christ figure in the novels, surely isn't safe, but he's good. More than that, he's great and mighty. He cannot dissociate from the stream any more than light can dissociate from the sun. It's the Lion's stream. His residing presence is what makes it flow. It runs at the beckoning of his call and according to the requisites of his terms. Jill need not fear the act of stooping before the Lion, only the tragic repercussions of passing up the offer. She may not like the terms of her drinking, but they were never hers to set. Either she drinks and finds abundant goodness at the Lion's feet or she passes over and continues a futile search for a nonexistent substitute.

Such is our quest for satisfaction. Like Jill, you can offer any variety of excuses to not drink from the stream. But know that your excuses will not alter the stream's flow nor the Lion's claim to stay beside it. Your excuses won't rob the stream of its ability to satisfy; it only robs you of its satisfying taste. You can choose to not stoop. You can refuse to find rest at its flowing side. You can choose to pass by and keep searching. But know that there will be no satisfying drink, no restful respite, no longing fulfilled at another stream. That's not because other streams can't offer what you're looking for but because there is no other stream to find. Either you drink and are filled in Christ's satisfying stream or you lose yourself in searching for a ghost of an alternative.

You don't have to drink from the stream—Christ, the Fountain of Living Water. Just know that if you do not drink from His stream, you will not drink at all. There is no satisfaction in any other source, no fulfillment from any other fountain, and no peace from any other stream. There is, in fact, no other stream at all.

~ *appendix a* ~
GOD'S WILL FOR YOUR LIFE

I n 2024, Billie Eilish's heartfelt ballad "What Was I Made For" took the world by storm. Written for the massively successful *Barbie* movie, the song won multiple Grammys, VMA Awards, and even an Oscar. As of November 2024, the song has been streamed over a billion times.

Though beautifully composed and hauntingly delivered, the song's power is in its relatability. Even though it's written about a fictional toy's existential crisis, there is something all too familiar. Who hasn't wondered what their purpose is? I know I have, many times over. I've yet to meet someone who *isn't* asking that question in their life, even if they don't recognize that they're asking it.

While we've already answered this question in very generic terms (see Chapters One and Two), I recognize that most of the time our asking for purpose is in search of the specific. We are asking what it is we should be specifically doing with our lives to give us fulfillment and satisfy our purpose. We want to know what job we should be working, who we ought to marry, what we are to study, or where we are to live. We are looking for details and direction.

While no one person or study can offer the answers to these questions, God has given us enough insight from the Scriptures to put us on the right track. In terms of America's pastime, this guide may not put you on first base, but it can help you determine which pitches to swing at while in the batter's box. So if you, like Barbie and Billie Eilish, are in desperate search of what you were made for, take heart and read on.

God's Worst-Kept Secret

If you've ever watched any of the *Bigfoot* hunting shows, you have probably picked up on the fact that each episode is pretty much the same. Some cohort of Bigfoot experts isolate themselves overnight in the backwoods of Oklahoma where there has been a recent "sighting." At some point in every episode, there is a mention of some elusive clue or vague evidence. There is always an intriguing footprint, a night-vision-filtered camera blur, or a strange wilderness call. The problem is that these clues never lead to verifiable evidence. They always go unresolved and fail to convince us. The show is strategically presented as a never-ending chase. Without the chase, there wouldn't be a show. In many ways, it's as if the chase itself has become more the prize than the object that is being chased.

In an uncomfortably similar way, that illustrates well how most young adults think of God's will. They view it as some mystical object that everyone is hoping is out there somewhere but no one really has a map to it. We search. We read. We pray. We seek advice. We take BuzzFeed quizzes. And maybe we get a glimpse. Maybe we get a little direction. But it never feels like we see the whole picture. We may get a footprint, but we never get to see the beast. God's will feels like it is one big, elusive secret—a secret we never get in on.

But what if we've misunderstood the whole conversation? What if God's will isn't some mythical beast always evading our night-vision cameras? Yes, God has a sovereign will that is often unseen by man. He has a transcendent will that is declared and fulfilled by Himself without human approval or assistance. After all, He is God, and He is sustaining every molecule that exists, every heartbeat of humanity, and every event in history. But what most people are seeking isn't God's will for the nations but His will for us individually. We want to know what God desires *of* and *from* our lives.

The very simple truth is that finding His will isn't nearly as elusive as we've made it out to be. He has actually made it abundantly clear; we just have to know where to look. If it's a secret, it must be the worst-kept secret. God's Word has made very plain what His will is for your life and for mine. It can be summarized in the following four points.

To Live Eternally (John 6:40)

God desires for you to live eternally. Jesus says it clearly when He declares that the Father's will is that all who look to the Son and believe should have everlasting life. Knowing and owning eternal life in Christ is the core of God's will for your life.

To some this may sound like a cop-out, but it's not. It's foundational. If you don't have this part down, the rest is irrelevant. God's will cannot be known or achieved apart from knowing Jesus. He is most interested not in what we spend our lives doing but in who we spend our lives knowing—namely, that we know Him.

And don't forget what we've already discovered in our study on satisfaction, that what is eternal is ultimate. What ultimate good is it to know what I'm supposed to do for the next two decades but then miss out on God's plan for the next two millennia into eternity? None! That would be like planning every detail of a two-hour layover at an airport only to get to your destination with nowhere to go, no place to stay, and nothing to do. Here is the beautifully liberating truth. If you only discover God's will for your eternity, that is enough—even if you never get the miraculous sign about where to take your career, or you never see the writing in the sky about who to marry. If all you know of what God desires is what relates to heaven, then you know enough to be satisfied. In eternity future, the chronological blimp of this present lifetime will seem very insignificant. What matters most is that you are prepared for the destination, not the layover on your way to it.

This isn't to suggest that today doesn't matter. It does, massively so. Primarily that is because what we do today impacts our eternity. Yet in our chase for purpose and knowing God's will, we must not dismiss the elementary insight of being destined to an eternity with Christ. This isn't merely an important piece of the puzzle; it is the whole puzzle.

To Live Gratefully (1 Thess. 5:18)

God's will for your life is that you learn to live with an attitude of gratitude. I know this truth likely lets you down a little bit. You were probably hoping for advice on which career to choose, and here I am talking about learning to say thank you. But don't bow out just yet. Consider the treasure hidden in this unassuming treasure chest. Paul tells us in 1 Thessalonians 5:18 that God's will for us is to give thanks in every circumstance, at all times and in all things—to live gratefully. This is God's will for you, that you have abundant, circumstance-transcending gratitude in your life.

It may not seem like much, but consider the power of this kind of gratitude. It has the potential to absolutely transform your life. What happens in your heart, your outlook, and your disposition if you are intentionally filled with and guided by gratitude every day of your life? Perhaps the things that often tease our discontentment (and with it our dissatisfaction) would begin to be powerless in our lives. Gratitude, as a disposition, teaches us to rest in what is good rather than stress about what is not. Gratitude reminds our grumblings that the car we drive, the ability to drive it, and the gas we can afford to fuel it matter more than the traffic we endure while sitting in it. Gratitude reminds our envy that we are far too materially blessed to waste any time wanting more stuff that we don't need. Gratitude reminds our worry that the God who has sustained us every moment of our life so far will not fail to do so going forward. Gratitude may not inform you of the details of the life you will lead, but it can transform the *kind* of life you live regardless of those details.

Ironically, our pursuit of God's will in our lives often produces discontentment and a lack of gratitude. We might become so obsessed with discovering the unrevealed that we fail to appreciate all that God has made clear. Just for moment, consider this. If you never find a career that satisfies your calling or if you wake up every day and perform menial tasks that don't seem to change the world but you remain thoroughly grateful for the goodness and grace of God in your life, you have successfully lived in God's will for your life. Isn't that liberating? Your gratitude is His will. Don't minimize the power of grateful living.

To Live Honorably (1 Pet. 2:15)

God also desires that you live honorably. Peter wrote in 1 Peter 2:15 to diligently engage in goodness or righteousness so the foolish in our world can have no reason to speak ill of your faith or lifestyle. Your life ought to be lived so honorably that by your testimony, the foolish cannot speak ignorantly of the God you serve or condescendingly of the life you lead.

This honorable living entails a few things. First, it means contending for personal purity in your life. While the overall thrust of the text is a commendation of our public testimony, it's a testimony that depends on our personal purity. It's living honorably by diligently seeking to do what is right in our hearts, in our heads, and with our hands—consistently, privately, publicly, faithfully. It's doing what honors the Lord and aligns with His Word.

Second, and going hand-in-hand with the first, living honorably means guarding your public testimony. As we seek to honor the Lord with our actions, we produce a testimony amidst a lost world and declare the goodness, glory, and grace of the Lord who has called us to such a lifestyle. That includes behaving with conviction, grace, benevolence, submission to authority, mercy, and godliness.

Peter offered this instruction to an exiled church that was experiencing deep persecution from nonbelievers. He knew that the greatest apologetic for Christianity is a Christian's honorable lifestyle. People might be able to contend with our theology, but they cannot argue about our actions. They can confess that Christianity is not true, but our lifestyle ought to remove the possibility that they will confess that it's not good.

Again, how liberating a grace is this good news. Whether you are the sought-after CEO or the overlooked janitor, whether you are the happily married or the life-long single, whether you own the picket-fence dreamhouse or spend your life signing leases that fill other people's pockets—you can live honorably for the Lord in the sight of the world. This is God's will for you.

To Live Purely (1 Thess. 4:1–8)

Complementing the command to live honorably, Paul further reveals that God's will is specifically that we would live purely—sanctified—in a world of sin. In context, Paul is specifically speaking of sexual purity. God's will is that we should control our bodies, our lusts, and our urges, and instead strive for holiness. We should never be charged with exploitation or sexual immorality.

It seems strange that God would make this particular area of sin a specific subsection of His will. Western 21st century culture has probably already taught you to be at odds with the biblical teaching on sex and sexuality. From the Jonas Brothers' purity-ring saga to the normalization of sexual dialogue in the sitcoms we watch, the Bible's mandates are often framed as outdated and unwanted. But even if you affirm the biblical position and boundaries of sexuality, why does God specifically include this on the short list of things to reveal about His will? Isn't it already covered in the living honorably category? And what makes sexual sin worth specific attention above other areas of sin?

Paul's elaboration in 1 Thessalonians seems to hold the answers. He reminds us of a few important things. First, God demands sexual purity because it possesses a testimonial distinction. That's what it means to be sanctified—to be set apart in holiness, to be unlike the wickedness around you. And one of the most obvious ways to do this is in regard to sexual activity. In a world obsessed with sex, lust, and pleasure, we are called to self-control, discipline, and the boundaries of God's beautiful design for sex. Sexual purity isn't just a battleground for our holiness; it's also a platform for our testimony.

Second, Paul argues that we must pursue God's will in purity out of consideration for the communal repercussions. We are reminded that for those who belong to the body of Christ, our sin impacts the rest of the body we are connected to. This is true of our sexual sin, whether it is hidden or not. There are consequences in our life and to those around us. In sexual immorality, our purity is never the only casualty.

Every time a young man or young woman has sex before they are married, they are robbing someone's future husband or wife of their virginity. For every cheating wife, there is a broken husband. Every man or woman on a screen being viewed for sexual pleasure is an image-bearer of God whose value is debased by our objectification. Sexual sin has far-reaching repercussions, which is why it is God's will that we separate from it.

If you are being honest with yourself, there is a good chance you have already failed to live in God's will for your life in this area. Whether it's premature sexual activity, porn addictions, or simply the unguarded thoughts you allow in your mind, you likely know well the failure of purity. And this failure may come with overwhelming shame, despair, or hopelessness. You may even feel that God's standard is unfair. After all, He created sex and sexuality. He's also placed us in a world obsessed with it. Why should He expect us to follow such supposedly outdated instructions? But can I remind you that God's instruction is always intended to maximize the fullness of life and never to rob you of it. He isn't looking to make you miserable by His boundaries but to make you free to enjoy the fullness of life to be had within them. That includes sexuality.

Also, don't forget that God's grace is always sufficient to redeem and restore. You may have failed a hundred times over in this department. You may feel like all hope is lost and you've ruined any chance at honoring God and living in His will for you. But that isn't true. The grace that flows from the cross of Christ is greater than your sin that has been nailed to it. If you will be diligent to confess your sin to Him, He will be faithful and just to forgive you (1 John 1:9).

Of course, purity is much more extensive than just sex. Although Paul's writing focuses primarily on sexuality, the lifestyle of purity we have been called to should permeate every area of our lives. And this purity is what God has in mind for you. It is His will for you.

So How Does This Help Me?

I know. I know. You were hoping God's will was going to be a little less obvious and a little more specific. But this is exactly why it's so important to work through His Word on this topic. God's revealed will is only disappointing to those who are looking for the wrong thing. You want to know what to do with your life, but God's will seems to be much more concerned with *who you are in your living* rather than *what you do for a living*.

God is so much more concerned about your character than He is your career. He cares more that you are godly than whether you are wealthy. He cares more for the manner of your living than He does the context of it. He cares more about who you are becoming than He does the details of what you spend your life doing.

There is much more to discuss (see Appendix B) regarding God's purpose for you, including specific details and direction. But don't skip ahead too quickly. Walking in His revealed will is the essential foundation for discovering His specific plan for your life. If you begin leaning toward any way of life that contradicts these four declarations of His will, rest assured that you are out of God's will for your life. Don't worry about discovering what He hasn't revealed as much as walking in what He has revealed. Start with the obvious while seeking the unspecified. If you aren't doing the first, forget about the second.

Find encouragement in these truths. People often spend their lives searching for some "Bigfoot" version of God's will. The truth is, following His will for your life is as simple as obeying these commands in Scripture. These four declarations of God's will shouldn't feel like a side-step to the main quest; they are the main quest. That means without knowing every detail of your future, you can walk today in God's will for your life.

~ *appendix b* ~
GOD'S PURPOSE FOR YOUR LIFE

W e've elaborated on the oh-so-evasive will of God, and now it's important to turn our conversation to God's purpose for our lives. Knowing now what God expects of us and from us, we can consider what God intends to do in us and through us.

I don't mean to further complicate an already complicated subject, and I certainly recognize that there is more to say than can be said in an appendix. But if we are going to look at the subject of purpose, we need to do it as much justice as possible. Based on the truths of Scripture and the simple observation of how it applies to our lives, we can now distinguish between God's general purpose for us and His specific purpose for us. We all have both a general purpose and a specific purpose. God's general purpose is that which has been revealed in God's Word for all of mankind throughout all time. It applies to every man and every woman who has ever been born and is a general reality true of all people in all places at all times. On the other hand, God's specific purpose (somewhat synonymous with the idea of "calling") refers to that which specifically relates to your life and how you apply God's general purpose. This purpose relates exclusively to you and what God is wanting to do in and through you.

In most people's search for purpose, they are looking for the specific purpose for their life. But it is essential that we understand both since they complement and depend on each other. What I've attempted to do is synthesize all this information and provide it to you in four essential steps. Consider it a guide as you chase after your purpose.

1. Search in the Right Place

Picture a fork in your mind. It can be any fork, any size, and any color—just a fork. Now for just a second, I want you to imagine that you are seeing a fork for the very first time. They don't exist in your world, so you are unaware of what this pronged object is. You're just going along with your best friend one day, and all of the sudden, this thing—a fork—appears. You had just been looking at *all your stuff.* You were thinking how all of it *was pretty neat.* You might consider that your *collection is complete.* People may even *think you're a girl, a girl who has everything.* (Okay, so maybe I'm telling you to imagine an early scene from *The Little Mermaid.* Stick with it.)

Imagine you find this fork and take it to the only person you know who can answer the mystery. His name is Scuttle, and he just so happens to be a seagull. So you swim up to the water's surface (you're a mermaid princess, remember?) and you show Scuttle your new relic. He says, "Oh yes. This is very rare. I can't believe you found it." He goes on to tell you that this fork is a "dinglehopper." He explains that a dinglehopper is a fancy tool used by humans to fix their hair. You just place it in your hair, twirl it around, and bam! Beautiful hair.

I remember when I first watched this scene as a kid. Even as a child, I knew that Scuttle was dramatically and hilariously wrong. He didn't really know the name of the object, and he didn't know what it was used for. But even though I knew he was obviously ignorant, Ariel believed him. She didn't know any better. It comes back to embarrass her later in the movie when she uses a dinner fork to comb her hair in front of her prospective lover.

May I suggest that even though it's great entertainment for a kid's movie, it's a tragically accurate representation of most people's pursuit of their purpose. Everyone has questions about their purpose and calling. We hold up this idea, this notion of purpose, and we look around asking, "Who can tell me what it is?" We end up going to all sorts of wrong places for the answer.

Tragically, the world is full of Scuttles. All sorts of people will try to tell you what your purpose is. They will tell you why you exist. "You exist for pleasure. You exist to get wealthy. You exist to make a difference in the world. You exist to find love. You exist to do whatever you want. You exist for no purpose at all." But what if the people you are listening to aren't qualified to answer the question? What if they are just as confused about it as you are?

The truth is, there is only one person who gets to declare what your purpose is in life. Only one person gets to decide and declare what the intention behind your existence is. Spoiler alert: it's the very God who brought you into existence and continues to keep you there. It's not that He has *a right* to determine your purpose; He has the *only right*. His role as purpose-giver is demanded by His creative work (Col. 1:16) and secured by His transcendent nature (Rom. 11:33–36).

Your mom may love you, but she doesn't get to define your purpose. Your professor may be a genius, but purpose-determiner isn't part of their title. Your boyfriend or girlfriend may know well what it means to cherish you, but that doesn't qualify them to define you or your reason for existing. If we are to ever discover what our purpose is in life, we must learn to search in the right place for the answers. Asking the right people is just as important as asking the right questions. And the truth is, your purpose in life does not exist and cannot be found apart from the God who made you.

2. Set the Right Filter

We live in a filter-obsessed world. Nearly every picture we take, every movie we make, every online post we place has been run through a catalogue of filters in search of the one that best accentuates what we want to see. In fact, selecting the right filter can be a tedious, time-consuming task because we know that filter determines perception. What we view an image through impacts our interpretation of the image itself.

The simple truth is that if we are to correctly see and understand our purpose, we must learn to view it through the right filter, which I adamantly contend is God's Word. If God is the only One with the right to define our purpose, we must learn to see ourselves through the lens of what He has said about us and to us. To put it plainly, if you do not look at your purpose through the lens of God's Word, you will not see your purpose correctly.

When we look in God's Word, we discover that even though it may not give us exact details of our specific purpose, it does tell us what God's general purpose is for us. And God's general purpose revealed in His Word is the filter by which we must see His specific purpose for our life. His specific purpose will never run contrary to or out of sync with His general purpose.

His general purpose—that which He has objectively made every human being for the sake of accomplishing—is divided into these two categories: (a) His purpose for us in creation and (b) His purpose for us in Christ. In the Garden of Eden, God had very specific plans for humanity. Though the plan appeared to have been jeopardized by sin, we know that God also had very specific plans for humankind in sacrificing His Son. It was an event in history that came as no mere afterthought but as the very centerpiece of the narrative.

In creation, our purpose is threefold: (1) to declare His glory by reflecting His image (Gen. 1:26–27), (2) to declare His goodness by demonstrating dominion (Gen. 1:26, 28–30), and (3) to declare His grace by living in relationship with Him (Gen. 3:8). That is why humans exist in creation. They are to declare His glory, His goodness, and His grace. That is why we exist. That is why *you* exist, to make known His glory, goodness, and grace.

Additionally, in Christ we have a greater purpose in redemption. This redeemed purpose is fourfold: (1) to be reconciled to God (1 Pet. 3:9, 2 Cor. 5:18), (2) to be reconcilers of others (2 Cor. 5:18, Matt. 28:19–20), (3) to be members of the body of Christ, the Church (1 Cor. 12, Heb. 10:25), and (4) to be doers of good works (Eph. 2:10). These are generally but objectively true of every believer in Christ. That is our purpose in Christ.

I understand the preceding two paragraphs have a lot of undeveloped content. I essentially opened a fire hydrant and asked you to drink it through a straw. While we don't have time to dive into each point, when we look at them from a big-picture perspective, the image begins to sharpen. Between His general purpose as revealed in creation and His redemptive purpose revealed in Christ, the meta-narrative of our life begins to take form. It can be summarized in this simple statement: You exist to know God deeply and to make Him known widely. That is your purpose, regardless of the school you attend, the career path you choose, or the person you marry. These are inescapable and overshadowing. This general purpose ought to be the filter through which you chase after your specific purpose.

So are you being faithful to these in your life? Are you seeking to accomplish what has been made abundantly clear in God's Word? Are you faithfully declaring His glory, His goodness, and His grace? Are you walking in reconciled fellowship with Him? Are you seeking to reconcile others to Him? Are you walking in godly community as you seek to live a life filled with righteousness and good works? If you aren't being faithful to your general purpose, what makes you think you are going to be faithful to His specific purpose? Your chase for the unknown must begin with faithfulness to the *already* known.

Observe the Right Signs

Having determined the right place to search and the right filter to look through, it's now essential that we learn to observe the right signs in our life. Our purpose comes with obvious signs and observable characteristics. The good news is this: God has designed you with a specific purpose in mind. Much like a box of crayons, all the colors exist for the same general purpose—to be pressed against paper and provide color to a bland world. However, each specific color is to be used at different times and in different ways to accomplish different feats, even if all of it is on the same canvas and contributing to the bigger picture. We can now consider what specific color we are individually and to what end we will be used in the Artist's hand.

God has intentionally given you the specifications of your personality, design, and experiences so you might fulfill His specific purpose for your life. Consider these traits a series of signs along the road. As long as you are paying attention, you'll end up where you are supposed to be.

What are these signs we should be looking for? The most helpful description I know comes from Rick Warren's bestselling book *The Purpose Driven Life*. In it, Warren coins a now-famous acronym—SHAPE—that helps define what we are looking for.

    S - Spiritual Gifts

    H - Heart/Passion

    A - Abilities

    P - Personality

    E - Experience

All five of these refer to areas of our life where God has sovereignly and intentionally overseen, designed, and provided for us certain traits or qualities that contribute to His overall, specific purpose for our life. Let's briefly consider each one.

Spiritual Gifts. If you have trusted God with your life and found grace, redemption, and forgiveness in Christ, then you have been given a spiritual gift—no exceptions, no exclusions. At the moment of our salvation, when the Holy Spirit of God indwells us as believers, He offers us gifts by which we are to serve the Church, the Body of Christ. While we don't have time to dive into a full discourse on spiritual gifts, I invite you to study 1 Corinthians 12, a good place to start reading what the gifts are and what they are for.

But the very inclusion of this gifting is significant. Most Christians think that since they aren't called to be a pastor or a missionary, their calling isn't spiritual. But that's simply not true. Although you may not be called to full-time, vocational ministry, you do still have a spiritual calling. God has gifted you through His Spirit to serve at a local church for a specific reason. If you are chasing your purpose but are neglecting to consider what that purpose looks like in the church, you're missing half of the point. Part of your calling is tied to serving God's people. Don't neglect that.

Heart/Passions: While I recognize the danger of using the word *heart* due to its overuse and misunderstanding in our culture, it's important that we consider this facet of our lives when looking for our purpose. What is meant by the word *passions* in this context isn't necessarily the emotional, intellectual, and willful center of our beings that the Bible calls desperately deceitful and sick (Jer. 17:9). Rather, it refers to what we naturally share deep concern for or interest in.

We all have things we are passionate about. But have you ever considered that God designed you with those passions intentionally? While our passions are never the foundation of our purpose, they can serve as helpful signs for identifying what our purpose is. The Scripture is full of passionate language from passionate people pursuing their God-given purpose. For example, when you read the Psalms, you never get the idea that David was writing from a place of obligation. He wasn't looking to top charts or entertain crowds. He was passionate about the honor that was due the Lord and the musical means by which it was given. God used such passion to accomplish great purposes throughout David's life.

Our interests can be any number of things. Your passion might be taking care of children, caring for people with special needs, understanding how the human body functions, ensuring judicial justice in our society, caring for animals, understanding how our universe operates, engineering new ways for things to function more effectively, finding cures for diseases, and more. There are countless passions the Lord might have laid on your heart. Pay attention to those and consider how they might give definition to your purpose.

Abilities: God has given you specific abilities and talents. Those giftings are indications of how He wants to use you specifically for His glory. Consider again King David's musical ministry. He was immensely talented with musical abilities. In fact, that was what the Lord used to open the door to the palace for David. Before he was crowned king, David served as a hired musician. Today, we still read and sing the songs David penned in worship to God. His talents were intentional, not accidental. They were a strategic means given by a strategic God to accomplish strategics ends.

However, also consider Moses for a moment. When God called him to be Israel's deliverer, Moses recognized his talent wasn't public speaking due to a vocal stutter. In fact, Moses actually requested that God pick another man for the job. God responds by telling Moses that his brother, Aaron, would help him with speaking. That begs the question: If Aaron were more gifted in what was needed, why didn't God just choose Aaron? And here is the beautiful answer. It is because although God is intentional with our abilities, He is not limited by our inabilities.

Don't worry if you aren't good at everything. In truth, nobody is a true jack of all-trades. God can still use you. Take what you are good at and use it for His glory.

Personality: God also gives us individual personalities. Some people are introverts. Some people are extroverts. Some people are thinkers. Some people are doers. Some people are planners. Some people are movers. None of this is by accident. All of it is by design.

Think of Peter, the hotheaded disciple who seemed to be overly dramatic and looking for a fight. While there were times it served as his vice, in the book of Acts it was this very boldness that God used to fuel the flame of the early Church. God designed him that way for that purpose in that time of history.

Don't get me wrong. That doesn't excuse any failures in character or integrity in our personalities that have been broken and distorted by sin. But God, in His goodness, still redeems and works through them despite our brokenness. So when searching for your purpose, be sure to consider your personality and the way God has specifically wired you.

Experience: Finally, God uses our experiences to help prepare and execute His purpose in our life. Think of Joseph in the Old Testament. He experienced great trials in slavery, false accusations, wrongful imprisonment, and abandonment by family and friends, but God was still working out His purpose in the midst of it all. It was through these experiences that God placed him in the right place at the right time to save his family from starvation and preserve the covenant promise God made to Abraham.

Or consider the blind man in the Gospels. When the disciples asked Jesus if the man was blind because of his own sin or because of his parents' sin, Jesus powerfully explained that it was neither. No one was at fault for the man's blindness. Rather, he was born blind so God might do an incredible work in His life and be glorified.

Your experiences are part of your purpose. For some of you, that might be hard to believe. You have experienced incredibly difficult events in your life. You carry trauma, stress, or wounds from horrible experiences. Perhaps you are still working through them. My goal isn't to minimize their severity but to encourage you despite the suffering they may have brought. God can and will use even your darkest days. Your experiences are part of His good plan. Trust that. Trust Him. And recognize that His purpose for you includes redeeming every experience for His glory.

When pursuing your purpose, make sure you are looking for the right signs. God has designed you with and redeemed you to very intentional traits, giftings, and experiences. Be sure to consider how all of them factor into His purpose for your life. And as you do, consider one final thing.

Aim for the Right Prize

Matthew 25 records a parable about a wealthy master who leaves some of his servants in charge of his possessions while he goes away for an extended season. No one knows where the master has gone or for what business he has departed. But one thing is certain. The master will return.

Upon his return, he demands an exact account of how each servant stewarded his possessions. Two of the servants had taken the portion they had been entrusted, invested it in other operations, and accrued a healthy additional sum for their master. One servant, however, had taken the entrusted goods and buried them for their safety. He had nothing more to give his master, only what had been originally left with him.

The point of the parable is that we are to be the wise stewards who invest what we've been entrusted with while we wait for the return of our King. And it's in this parable that we find the famous commendation that Christians so often reference. "Well *done*, good and faithful servant" (Matt. 25:21). That is the goal we strive for, to be found faithful when the King returns.

Perhaps we've gotten it backward. Maybe instead of chasing the frustratingly elusive idea of purpose we ought to be chasing faithfulness. Maybe purpose doesn't precede faithfulness, but it's in our pursuit of faithfulness that our purpose is revealed. The truth is that when your objective is faithfulness, you will never miss your purpose. Your purpose can be summarized in that all-encompassing refrain: "Well *done*, good and faithful servant." What in your life would be different if you spent more time securing the "well done" of your Master instead of the secrets of His plan? What would happen if you started living for a better prize?

Onward to His Plan

Having one hand firmly grasping God's declared will and the other firmly grasping His declared and designed purposes, we can begin to wrestle with the details of God's specific plan for our individual lives. His will informs His purposes, and together they form His plan.

At no point will God's plan for you lead you outside the parameters of His declared will and declared purposes. So if you begin to entertain a lifestyle or lean toward a decision that is clearly contradictory to any one of these points, you can rest assured that it's not from God and it's not for you. These truths serve as the map by which you chart your course. If there is a path it doesn't account for, don't be foolish enough to walk down it. Know His will, rest in His purposes, be faithful to His design in your life, and trust Him for the details that are yet to be seen.

Note: I recognize these two appendixes have traversed a wide variety of ground. To help synthesize it all, I've included an illustrated graphic of the material we've covered in Appendix A and Appendix B. I've found it to be a helpful reference for both my own life and in the encouragement of others. May it be a faithful friend to you as well.

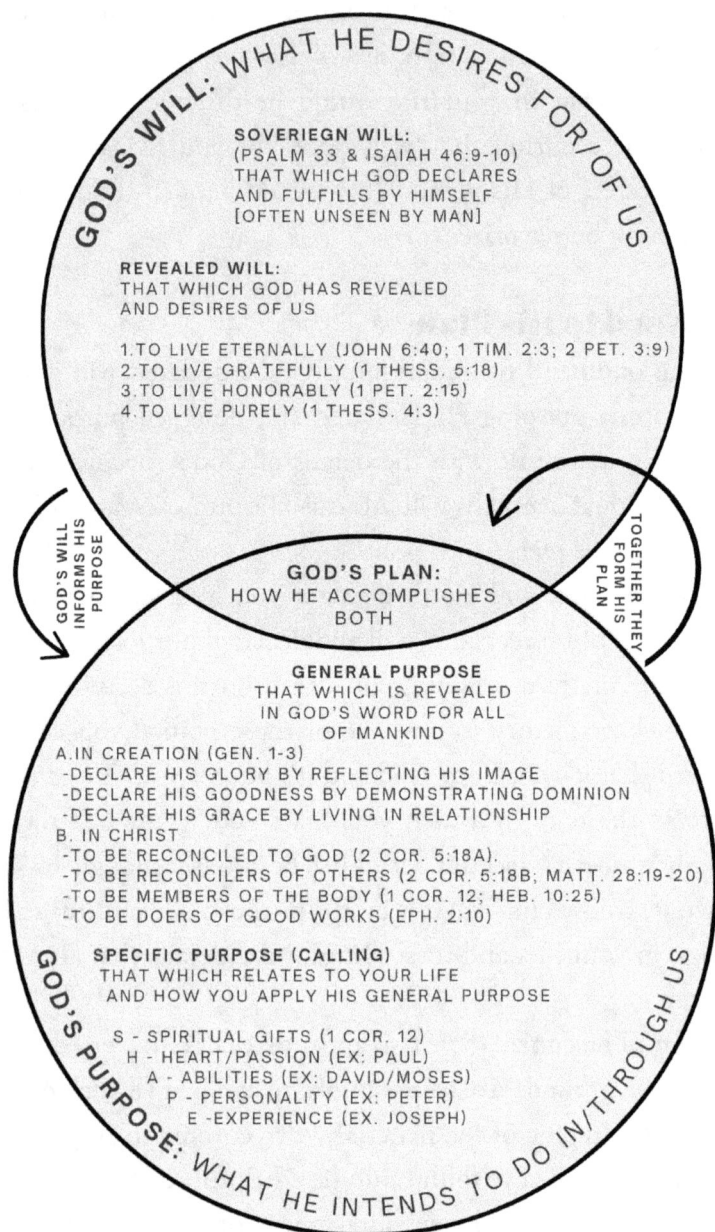

GOD'S WILL: WHAT HE DESIRES FOR/OF US

SOVERIEGN WILL:
(PSALM 33 & ISAIAH 46:9-10)
THAT WHICH GOD DECLARES
AND FULFILLS BY HIMSELF
[OFTEN UNSEEN BY MAN]

REVEALED WILL:
THAT WHICH GOD HAS REVEALED
AND DESIRES OF US

1. TO LIVE ETERNALLY (JOHN 6:40; 1 TIM. 2:3; 2 PET. 3:9)
2. TO LIVE GRATEFULLY (1 THESS. 5:18)
3. TO LIVE HONORABLY (1 PET. 2:15)
4. TO LIVE PURELY (1 THESS. 4:3)

GOD'S WILL INFORMS HIS PURPOSE

TOGETHER THEY FORM HIS PLAN

GOD'S PLAN:
HOW HE ACCOMPLISHES
BOTH

GENERAL PURPOSE
THAT WHICH IS REVEALED
IN GOD'S WORD FOR ALL
OF MANKIND
A. IN CREATION (GEN. 1-3)
  -DECLARE HIS GLORY BY REFLECTING HIS IMAGE
  -DECLARE HIS GOODNESS BY DEMONSTRATING DOMINION
  -DECLARE HIS GRACE BY LIVING IN RELATIONSHIP
B. IN CHRIST
  -TO BE RECONCILED TO GOD (2 COR. 5:18A).
  -TO BE RECONCILERS OF OTHERS (2 COR. 5:18B; MATT. 28:19-20)
  -TO BE MEMBERS OF THE BODY (1 COR. 12; HEB. 10:25)
  -TO BE DOERS OF GOOD WORKS (EPH. 2:10)

SPECIFIC PURPOSE (CALLING)
THAT WHICH RELATES TO YOUR LIFE
AND HOW YOU APPLY HIS GENERAL PURPOSE

S - SPIRITUAL GIFTS (1 COR. 12)
H - HEART/PASSION (EX: PAUL)
A - ABILITIES (EX: DAVID/MOSES)
P - PERSONALITY (EX: PETER)
E - EXPERIENCE (EX: JOSEPH)

GOD'S PURPOSE: WHAT HE INTENDS TO DO IN/THROUGH US

GROUP DISCUSSION GUIDE

Introduction

- What personal experiences of disappointment or dissatisfaction resonate with the text? How have those experiences shaped your perspective on life?
- Have you ever found yourself in a "ruinous labyrinth" as described by John Calvin? What was it, and how did you try to navigate through it?
- Why do you think Millennials and Gen Zers are reportedly the least satisfied generations, despite living in an era of technological advancement and global connectivity?
- Do you agree with the notion that young adulthood has become a trial phase for experimentation and self-discovery? How does this idea influence personal decisions and societal norms?
- The text challenges the idea that life's satisfaction can be found in doing what makes you happy. Do you agree or disagree with that statement? Why?
- What does the text suggest about the relationship between cultural messages (e.g., do what makes you happy) and the rise of dissatisfaction among younger generations?
- How does the concept of Jesus offering the fullness of life change the way you view life's disappointments or unmet expectations?

Chapter One

- Have you ever found yourself chasing something that seemed important at the time, only to realize later that it wasn't what you truly needed or wanted? How did you respond?

- The author mentions the concept of "chasing the wrong Uber." What are some examples of "wrong Ubers" people pursue in their lives?

- The story highlights an initial sense of excitement that turned into disappointment. Why do you think fleeting excitement often blinds us to deeper needs or priorities?

- In Jeremiah 2:13, God refers to Himself as the "fountain of living waters" and contrasts this with broken cisterns. What does this metaphor mean to you? How does it relate to your daily life?

- The author ties the human desire for satisfaction to the pursuit of God. Do you agree that fulfillment can only be found in God? Why or why not?

- C. S. Lewis stated, "We are far too easily pleased." How does this idea challenge the way we approach satisfaction and happiness in life?

- The text suggests that many people settle for "mud pies" instead of seeking the "holiday at the sea." What are some "mud pies" you see in our culture today? Why do people settle for them?

- What does true satisfaction mean to you? How does it differ from temporary pleasures or achievements?

- The story ends with an invitation to pursue better sources of satisfaction. What practical steps can we take to avoid settling for less in our personal or spiritual lives?

- How do societal pressures or expectations contribute to people chasing after the wrong things? Can you think of examples where this happens in your own community?
- Have you ever had a moment when helping someone else gave you clarity about your own priorities or life direction? Share your experience.
- The author mentions that young adulthood is a particularly challenging time to find direction. How can we encourage and support each other in pursuing meaningful goals and lasting satisfaction?

Chapter Two

- What are some "empty wells" people turn to for fulfillment today? How do they compare to the woman at the well's search for satisfaction?
- The text discusses Jesus breaking cultural boundaries to interact with the Samaritan woman. What can we learn from His approach when interacting with people who are different from us?
- Why do you think the Samaritan woman initially tried to disguise her brokenness from Jesus? What does that tell us about human nature and vulnerability?
- Jesus intentionally addressed the woman's past rather than avoiding it. Why is it important to confront our pain and failures in order to experience true healing?
- The text describes how the woman deferred her spiritual hopes to a future Messiah but failed to recognize Jesus when He was right in front of her. How can we avoid missing what God is doing in our lives in the present?

- The story highlights Jesus's ability to satisfy the deepest longings of the heart. What does "living water" symbolize for you personally? How have you experienced it or sought it?
- The text states, "Our quest for satisfaction starts and ends with Jesus." How does this statement challenge or affirm your current view of fulfillment and purpose in life?
- In what ways does the message of the Samaritan woman apply to people who feel excluded or unworthy today? How can we communicate to them Jesus's offer of living water?
- How does this passage shape your understanding of God's grace and His willingness to meet us where we are, no matter our past?

Chapter Three

- The author describes a humorous memory of being gullible. Can you share a personal experience where you believed something outrageous? What did you learn from it?
- Why do you think people are naturally skeptical of big promises? How does that apply to both everyday interactions and spiritual beliefs?
- The author emphasizes that trust is born out of familiarity. How does this idea relate to your relationships with others or with God?
- Jonathan Edwards said, "Men will trust in God no further than they know Him." How do you interpret that statement? What practical steps can we take to grow in our knowledge of God?
- The text discusses being "made by" God versus being "made for" God. How do you think this distinction affects how we view our purpose in life?

- What does it mean to you that "God didn't create us with desires just to dangle their fulfillment out of our reach"? How do you reconcile that with unmet longings in life?
- How does the concept of being saved *to* something (e.g., a life of fullness and intimacy with God) differ from the idea of being saved merely *from* something?
- The text says Jesus offers abundant life, not just salvation from sin. How would you define abundant life? Is it something you're currently experiencing?
- Psalm 23 is often associated with peace and satisfaction. What stands out to you most about the metaphor of God as a Shepherd in your life?
- David's statement "I shall not want" suggests a deep level of contentment. Do you find that kind of satisfaction in God? If not, what hinders you?
- The text asked, "Have you made Him [God] your Shepherd?" How would you honestly answer that question? What might it look like to take steps toward doing so?
- The text concludes with the idea that "our longings prove deep, but He [God] proves to be a Well deeper still." How does that encourage or challenge you?

Chapter Four

- The author describes participating in a water well project in Central America. Have you ever been involved in a service project that impacted your perspective on privilege or need? How did it shape your understanding?
- The text emphasizes that knowing God personally is different from knowing about Him. How would you describe

the difference between those two concepts? Have you experienced that difference on your own faith journey?

- The text highlights the importance of choosing to delight in God, regardless of circumstances. How do you intentionally find joy in your relationship with God, especially during difficult times?
- Why do you think satisfaction in Christ is easier to affirm theologically than to live out practically? What practical steps can you take to bridge that gap?
- The author ties abiding in Christ to spiritual disciplines such as prayer, Scripture reading, and worship. Which of those disciplines do you find most challenging? Why? How can we encourage one another to remain consistent in them?
- The text contrasts experiencing satisfaction in Christ with merely observing it. What does it look like to truly "taste and see that the Lord is good" in everyday life?
- How can being part of a faith community help you abide in Christ and find satisfaction in Him? Share examples of how others have encouraged you in your faith.
- The author suggests that when we delight in God, our desires align with His will. How have you seen that principle play out in your own life or the lives of others?

Chapter Five

- What were some small but meaningful ways you and your friends passed the time in school? Did those activities teach you anything lasting?
- The text discusses how people often mistake external signs such as wealth or relationships for satisfaction. How do you

personally distinguish between true satisfaction and fleeting contentment in your life?

- Do you agree with the statement that people often chase "empty wells" of satisfaction? Can you share a time in your life when something you pursued didn't fulfill you as expected?

- In the section on contentment, Paul's declaration in Philippians 4 is a central concept. How does his example of being content in all circumstances challenge your perspective on gratitude or faith?

- What does "being content with what He [God] gives and not obsessed with what He hasn't" look like practically in your daily life? How can that mindset change how you approach struggles or unmet desires?

- The text emphasizes the importance of having the right "posture of the heart." How do you think our inner attitudes influence the way we respond to challenges or disappointments?

- Joy is described as more than just happiness. It's a steady confidence in Christ even during difficult times. How have you seen or experienced that kind of joy in your life or in someone else's?

- The metaphor of life as a "movie trailer" for heaven is vivid. How does viewing life that way reshape how you handle temporary frustrations or challenges?

- The text challenges us to consider whether we truly long for heaven. What does "eternal anticipation" look like for you, and how does it influence your choices or priorities now?

- The text argues that simple truths such as contentment and joy are foundational to Christian living but often overlooked. Why do you think simplicity can sometimes be undervalued in our spiritual lives?
- What practical steps can you take this week to cultivate more contentment, joy, or eternal anticipation in your daily life?

Chapter Six

- How do you interpret the phrase "actions speak louder than words" in the context of your personal faith or values?
- The text highlights that satisfaction in Christ begins in the heart but must be evident in your actions. How does that idea challenge or affirm your current lifestyle?
- What does "exclusive adoration" of God mean to you? How does it differ from the way society often uses the word *adore*?
- Psalm 63 describes God's love as "better than life." What are some practical ways we can reflect this level of satisfaction in our daily lives?
- The text connects rebellion with dissatisfaction. Have you ever experienced dissatisfaction leading to disobedience? What lessons did you learn from it?
- In Psalm 17:15, David speaks of satisfaction being tied to obedience. How do you reconcile the challenges of obedience with the promise of satisfaction?
- The Samaritan woman immediately shared her experience with Jesus despite her social status. How does that inspire you or challenge your approach to sharing your faith?

- The text suggests that sharing the good news is both a natural response to satisfaction and a test of it. How do you see that playing out in your life or in the lives of others?
- The text acknowledges that obedience to Christ can lead to social or personal difficulties. What strategies can we use to remain faithful when obedience is costly?
- Reflecting on the closing thoughts, how can moments of discouragement about a lack of "signs of satisfaction" in our lives bring us closer to God instead of pushing us away?

Conclusion

- The author admits to procrastinating on renewing his vehicle registration despite repeated reminders and even an attempt from the state to make it easier. Have you ever experienced a similar situation in which you willfully avoided what you knew you should be doing?
- The text highlights the difference between inconvenience and difficulty. How do you personally define the difference? Can you share an example of confusing the two in your life?
- The text compares stubbornness to this proverb: "You can lead a horse to water, but you can't make it drink." When have you found yourself acting like the "stubborn horse"? What changed your perspective? Was there someone in your life who showed incredible patience with you during that time?
- Have you ever been in a position where you were trying to guide someone to make better choices but they resisted? How did that affect you?

- The text states that many people in the world are succeeding in things that don't matter. What do you think qualifies as "things that matter"? How can we focus more on those things in our lives?

- The text encourages readers to "put it to the test" when evaluating spiritual claims. How open are you to testing beliefs? How do you approach investigating truth in your own life?

- What does the idea of foolishness as "a lack of investigation" mean to you? Can you recall a time when you dismissed something without giving it fair consideration?

- Jill's interaction with the Lion emphasizes that the Lion is not safe but good. What does that mean in relation to Christ? Why is that good news for us as His followers?

- In the *Narnia* excerpt, Jill hesitates to drink from the stream out of fear of the Lion. What fears or reservations might keep people from fully committing to their faith?

- The text states, "Your excuses won't rob the stream of its ability to satisfy; it only robs you of its satisfying taste." What excuses do people commonly use to avoid pursuing fulfillment or purpose? How do those excuses hold them back?

- The imagery of stooping to drink from the stream conveys both humility and surrender. How does that symbolism resonate with your own experiences of seeking fulfillment or purpose?

- How do you interpret the tension between the Lion's unwavering presence and the choice Jill has to drink or not? What does that teach us about the balance of free will and divine invitation?

Appendix A: God's Will for Your Life

- Billie Eilish's song speaks to the universal search for purpose. How do you personally connect with this idea of questioning your purpose? Can you recall a time when you've wrestled with the question, "What was I made for?"

- The text compares the search for God's will to chasing an elusive mystery like Bigfoot. Why do you think many people view God's will as something difficult to discover? Do you agree or disagree with that analogy? Why?

- The text emphasizes that knowing God's will for eternity is foundational. How does focusing on eternity change how we approach decisions about our careers, relationships, or daily life?

- The text highlights gratitude as a transformative practice central to God's will. What role does gratitude currently play in your life? How might practicing gratitude shift your perspective on challenges or unmet desires?

- The text suggests that living honorably includes both personal purity and a strong public testimony. How can our daily actions—no matter how small—impact the way others view Christianity? Can you share an example?

- The text delves into the significance of sexual purity as part of living within God's will. Why do you think God places such a strong emphasis on purity? How can we as individuals or a community better support each other in pursuing purity?

- The text suggests that many are disappointed by God's revealed will because they are "looking for the wrong thing." How does that statement resonate with you? What are some ways we might realign our desires with God's priorities?

- The text emphasizes God's concern with who we are over what we do. How does that perspective challenge or affirm your current understanding of success and purpose?
- Which of the four revealed aspects of God's will—living eternally, gratefully, honorably, and purely—do you find the most challenging? What practical steps could you take to grow in that area?
- The text claims that following God's revealed will is foundational to discovering the specifics of His plan. How might this perspective encourage someone who feels stuck or uncertain about their life's direction?

Appendix B: God's Purpose for Your Life

- The text differentiates between God's general purpose and specific purpose for our lives. How do those two concepts complement each other? Why is it essential to understand both?
- The text claims that "God is the only one with the right to define our purpose." How does that claim shape the way we should approach major life decisions?
- In the fork analogy from *The Little Mermaid*, Ariel seeks advice from someone unqualified. How can that story serve as a warning in our search for purpose? How do we recognize Scuttles in our own life?
- Why does the text emphasize the importance of searching for purpose through God's Word rather than the world's perspectives?
- The text states that God's specific purpose will never contradict His general purpose. Why is this principle significant when evaluating life's choices or opportunities?

- How does viewing life through the filter of God's Word help refine our understanding of our purpose? Can you think of examples where a lack of this filter has led to confusion?
- The SHAPE framework (Spiritual Gifts, Heart/Passion, Abilities, Personality, Experience) is presented as a guide to understanding specific purposes. Which of those five categories resonates most with your personal journey? Why? Have you taken the time to work through each of the five categories and identify your specifications within them?
- How can reflecting on past experiences, including painful ones, help us recognize God's purpose for our lives?
- The text suggests that pursuing faithfulness to God often leads to discovering purpose. How might this idea reshape common misconceptions about the search for purpose?
- What does it mean to "live for the better prize" (the commendation, "Well *done*, good and faithful servant")? How might adopting that perspective transform your daily living?
- The author states that "faithfulness to the already known" is foundational before pursuing the unknown. What areas in your life might require greater faithfulness as you seek clarity in God's specific plan?

ACKNOWLEDGMENTS

There are countless people who have invested in my life through the years and in turn made this book a reality. While I cannot possibly exhaust the list, there are a few individuals who deserve special praise for their partnership in this project.

To my wife, thank you for allowing me the time and space to write. I spent many hours and many nights distracted in thought or busy at a keyboard. You were patient. You were kind. You were understanding. You were an example of a Jesus-satisfied life. You were a ready sounding board and a willing aid. I am so undeserving but so grateful for you, one of God's greatest graces in my life. Thank you for being my partner, not only in writing this book but in life.

To my parents, thank you for believing in me and investing in this project with me. Unbeknownst to you, you shaped this book in so many ways. You may have not crafted a single sentence, but you spent a lifetime helping craft the one who wrote them. As such, I owe so much of my theology, my love for Jesus, my love for others, and my knowledge of His satisfaction to your faithful care and constant example.

To Rowan and Lochlan, thank you for motivating me in ways you will likely never comprehend.

To Lee Wallace, thank you for patiently and faithfully reading through each gathering section of this project. What started as a seminary assignment has blossomed into something much more. Thank you for your guidance and grace throughout this project.

To everyone who has ever been a part of our family at *The Well*, thank you for being the inspiration behind this book. The truths organized in these pages are the product of so many sermons, lessons, phone calls, and late Thursday night conversations after service. The notion of satisfaction in Christ isn't merely a lesson I long to impart to others; it's been a beautiful truth I've been able to behold in so many of your lives. This book isn't just for you–it's because of you. Keep showing the world that there is life in the Well.

To Aaron, Aimee, and Alex, thank you for being the best siblings anyone could ask for. You all have molded and sharpened me in ways I've never expressed enough appreciation for.

To Meghan Brenenstuhl, thank you for being a catalyst in the publishing process. Your kindness and excitement for this project brought me encouragement when I had mostly given up hope on it. You are an incredible cousin and an even more incredible follower of Jesus. You powerfully exemplify the life I contend for in this book.

To Tina Fagerberg and Kylie Jefferson, thank you for helping me look like a professional. We just may fool the world.

To everyone at Lucid Books, thank you for taking this project on and making this dream a reality. What a massive blessing you are to the literary world and to so many aspiring authors whose words deserve to be in print.

SOURCES

Ashman, Howard, and Alan Menken. "Part of Your World." Performed by Jodi Benson. *The Little Mermaid: Original Motion Picture Soundtrack.* Walt Disney Records, 1989.

Calvin, John. *Commentaries on the Catholic Epistles.* Translated by John Owen. Christian Classics Ethereal Library, 1855.

"Clean Drinking Water Update: 703 Million People Still Lack Access." Accessed January 20, 2025. https://madeblue.org/en/clean-water-update-771-million-people/.

Clements, Ron, and John Musker, Directors. *The Little Mermaid.* Produced by Howard Ashman and John Musker. Walt Disney Pictures, 1989.

"Deadpool and Wolverine Is Most Watched Trailer Ever." *Men's Journal.* Accessed January 20, 2025. https://www.mensjournal.com/streaming/deadpool-and-wolverine-is-most-watched-trailer-ever.

Edwards, Jonathan. *The Religious Affections.* Yale University Press, 1959.

Eilish, Billie. "What Was I Made For?" Recorded on *Barbie the Album*, July 21, 2023. Darkroom/Interscope Records.

Lewis, C. S. *Mere Christianity*. HarperCollins, 2001.

Lewis, C. S. *The Silver Chair*. HarperCollins, 1994.

Lewis, C. S. *The Weight of Glory*. Macmillan, 1949.

Piper, John. *Desiring God: Meditations of a Christian Hedonist*. Multnomah Publishers, 2003.

Powell, Alvin. "Why Are Young People So Miserable?" *Harvard Gazette*. September 15, 2022. https://news.harvard.edu/gazette/story/2022/09/why-are-young-people-so-miserable/.

Ridder, M. "Volume of Bottled Water in the United States from 2010 to 2023." *Statista*. January 8, 2025. https://www.statista.com/statistics/237832/volume-of-bottled-water-in-the-us/.

Spurgeon, Charles H. *The Treasury of David: An Expository and Devotional Commentary on the Psalms*. Passmore & Alabaster, 1885.

Thomas, I. D. E. *A Puritan Golden Treasury*. Banner of Truth, 2000.

Tozer, A. W. *The Attributes of God, Volume 1: A Journey into the Father's Heart*. WingSpread, 2006.

Warren, Rick. *The Purpose Driven Life: What on Earth Am I Here For?* Zondervan, 2002.